Paranoid Personality Disorder

Understanding, Coping, and Thriving Beyond the Shadows of Paranoia

By

Dr. Jordan Morgan

Contents

Chapter 15: Living a Full Life with Paranoid Personality Disorder.................273

Conclusion: A Final Word on Thriving Beyond Paranoia.................288

Copyright Page

Introduction

The Journey to Understanding Paranoid Personality Disorder

Paranoid Personality Disorder (PPD) is one of the lesser-discussed yet most perplexing mental health conditions. Often misunderstood and stigmatized, PPD is defined by an enduring pattern of mistrust and suspicion towards others. Individuals with PPD constantly feel that people around them have hidden motives, which leads to a guarded, defensive, and hostile worldview. This paranoia can affect every aspect of a person's life—relationships, work, and even basic day-to-day functioning. Understanding PPD requires a deep dive into not just the symptoms and diagnosis but also the emotional and psychological underpinnings that shape this disorder.

The journey to understanding PPD is one of unraveling a complex tapestry of cognitive distortions, emotional struggles, and interpersonal dynamics. It is a journey that delves into the human psyche to explore how deeply held beliefs and past experiences can distort reality. It is also a journey that highlights how PPD impacts not only the person suffering from it but also the people in their lives. To truly comprehend PPD, we must go beyond just the clinical symptoms and look into the lived experience of those who carry this condition daily.

This introduction sets the stage for a comprehensive understanding of PPD, shedding light on its origins, symptoms, and societal impact. From the initial awareness of the disorder to the practical steps for managing it, the aim is to provide a roadmap for both individuals diagnosed with PPD and their loved ones, offering strategies for coping, healing, and ultimately thriving despite the challenges this disorder presents.

Defining Paranoid Personality Disorder

At its core, Paranoid Personality Disorder is a mental health condition that is primarily characterized by chronic suspicion and mistrust of others. This pervasive pattern of distrust often leads individuals with PPD to perceive the actions and intentions of others as malevolent, even when no such ill intent exists. The mistrust is not just fleeting or temporary—it is a fundamental part of the individual's worldview, influencing every relationship and interaction.

According to the Diagnostic and Statistical Manual of Mental Disorders, Fifth Edition (DSM-5), the diagnostic criteria for PPD include behaviors such as:

- Suspecting, without sufficient basis, that others are exploiting, harming, or deceiving them.
- Preoccupation with unjustified doubts about the loyalty or trustworthiness of friends or associates.
- Reluctance to confide in others due to unwarranted fear that the information will be used maliciously.
- Reading hidden, threatening meanings into benign remarks or events.
- Persisting in holding grudges and being unforgiving.
- Perceptions of attacks on their character or reputation that are not apparent to others and are quick to react angrily or counterattack.

While the disorder is more prevalent in men, it can affect both genders, and its onset typically begins in early adulthood, often becoming more pronounced in social and work-related environments. Despite being diagnosed as a personality disorder, which by definition is long-lasting and pervasive, it is crucial to note that those with PPD are capable of functioning in society, though their interactions with others are often strained.

The challenging aspect of understanding PPD is that individuals with the disorder are often unaware of their distorted perceptions. Their reality is so deeply ingrained that they may not see their behavior as abnormal. Instead, they view themselves as merely cautious, protecting themselves from the world that they perceive as threatening. This profound sense of alienation and suspicion can lead to social isolation, difficulties in relationships, and even problems in maintaining steady employment.

The Historical Evolution of PPD Diagnosis

The concept of paranoia has existed for centuries, but the classification of Paranoid Personality Disorder as a distinct diagnosis is relatively recent. Historically, paranoia was often seen as a symptom of other mental illnesses, such as schizophrenia. It was not until the late 20th century that mental health professionals began to separate paranoia as a personality disorder in its own right.

In earlier diagnostic systems, paranoia was grouped under the umbrella term "psychosis," often associated with delusional thinking. The shift towards defining PPD as a personality disorder emerged from a growing understanding of the psychological underpinnings of paranoia. This move also highlighted the fact that paranoia could exist independently, not just as a symptom of other conditions like schizophrenia or mood disorders.

Over time, with the refinement of diagnostic criteria in the DSM, PPD became more clearly distinguished from other disorders that involve paranoia. Unlike psychotic disorders, PPD does not involve hallucinations or delusions but rather a long-standing pattern of suspicion and mistrust. This distinction was critical in providing individuals with the appropriate treatment and support tailored to their unique challenges.

As our understanding of PPD has evolved, so too has the approach to treatment. While early models focused heavily on managing the disorder with psychotherapy and medications, newer perspectives now advocate for a more holistic approach that involves coping mechanisms, mindfulness, and social support, allowing individuals to lead fulfilling lives despite their challenges.

Distinguishing PPD from Other Personality Disorders

PPD shares some symptoms with other personality disorders, particularly those in the Cluster A category (which includes Schizoid and Schizotypal Personality Disorders), but it is important to recognize its distinct characteristics. Cluster A personality disorders, often labeled as "odd or eccentric," are typified by behaviors that are not in line with conventional social expectations. While both Schizoid and Schizotypal disorders involve social detachment, PPD is specifically marked by an extreme sense of suspicion and fear of betrayal.

One of the key differentiators of PPD is that its symptoms stem from a fundamental mistrust of others, rather than a desire for social isolation or eccentric thinking. In contrast to Schizoid Personality Disorder, where individuals often show little interest in social interactions, those with PPD may seek relationships but sabotage them out of fear of exploitation. This fear often results in paranoia toward close friends, family, or coworkers, causing a strain on their relationships and social connections.

Additionally, unlike Borderline Personality Disorder (BPD) and Narcissistic Personality Disorder (NPD), which tend to involve more volatile emotional responses, the paranoia in PPD is typically stable over time, characterized more by constant vigilance rather than intense mood swings or fluctuations in self-esteem.

The distinctions between these disorders are crucial for proper diagnosis and treatment, as each requires a unique therapeutic approach. Misdiagnosis is common, especially because PPD's symptoms may overlap with other disorders, making it essential for mental health professionals to conduct a thorough assessment before arriving at a definitive diagnosis.

The Prevalence and Risk Factors

While the exact prevalence of Paranoid Personality Disorder is difficult to pinpoint, estimates suggest that about 2-4% of the general population may be affected by PPD. It is more common in men and typically becomes apparent in late adolescence or early adulthood. The onset is gradual, and many individuals may not seek treatment until their symptoms significantly interfere with their relationships or daily functioning.

Several risk factors contribute to the development of PPD. Family history plays a significant role—individuals who have close relatives with personality disorders or other mental health conditions are at a higher risk. Childhood trauma, especially emotional neglect or abuse, is another critical factor. Children who grow up in environments where mistrust is modeled or where they experience unpredictable or abusive treatment may develop a heightened sensitivity to betrayal, which can later evolve into PPD.

Environmental stressors, such as living in unsafe or threatening conditions, may also contribute to the development of the disorder. Furthermore, research indicates that individuals with PPD may have an increased sensitivity to social rejection or criticism, which can further perpetuate their feelings of alienation.

It is important to note, however, that not everyone with these risk factors will develop PPD. Genetics, environmental influences, and personal coping mechanisms all play a role in determining whether an individual will develop the disorder. Understanding these factors helps to better tailor interventions and prevention strategies for those at risk.

The Impact of Paranoia on Daily Life

The impact of Paranoid Personality Disorder is profound, affecting nearly every aspect of a person's life. One of the most noticeable effects is the way it disrupts relationships. Individuals with PPD often push others away because they believe that their loved ones or colleagues are out to deceive or harm them. They may interpret benign comments or actions as personal attacks, leading to frequent misunderstandings and conflicts.

At work, individuals with PPD may struggle with trusting coworkers, believing that others are scheming behind their backs. This constant suspicion can undermine job performance and make it difficult for them to collaborate or communicate effectively. The paranoia may even extend to authority figures or supervisors, leading to resistance to feedback or perceived threats to their job security.

Social isolation is another common consequence of PPD. Because of their inability to trust others, individuals with PPD often withdraw from social activities and avoid forming close relationships. This withdrawal can lead to feelings of loneliness and alienation, further intensifying their sense of paranoia.

Overall, PPD can severely hinder a person's ability to live a fulfilling life. The disorder creates a constant emotional burden, making it difficult to experience peace or contentment. However, with the right interventions, individuals with PPD can learn to manage their symptoms and lead fulfilling lives. The first step in this process is understanding the disorder—its origins, symptoms, and how it affects the individual and their relationships. This understanding is the foundation for effective coping strategies and treatment options that can empower individuals to navigate their world with greater clarity and confidence.

In the chapters that follow, we will delve deeper into the science behind PPD, treatment methods, and strategies for coping, healing, and thriving beyond the shadows of paranoia.

Chapter 1: The Anatomy of Paranoia

Paranoia, a term frequently associated with suspicion and wariness, often carries a stigma of irrationality or exaggerated caution. This oversimplified perception does little justice to the complex psychological processes at play. Paranoia, particularly as seen in Paranoid Personality Disorder (PPD), extends far beyond mere mistrust. It is a deeply ingrained and pervasive pattern of thinking, feeling, and behaving that can significantly affect a person's relationships, sense of security, and overall quality of life.

PPD is not merely a heightened sense of caution but a chronic and maladaptive state of mistrust and suspicion. It is characterized by an unrelenting belief that others are out to deceive, harm, or exploit. This disorder represents one of the Cluster A personality disorders, which are marked by eccentric or odd behavior. Understanding PPD requires an exploration of the intricate interplay between cognition, emotion, and environmental influences that shape this condition.

The roots of PPD often lie in the individual's interpretation of their experiences and their inherent need for self-preservation. This instinct, while crucial for survival, can become distorted, turning what might otherwise be reasonable caution into an overwhelming and debilitating worldview. The mechanisms of paranoia can vary widely among individuals, influenced by genetic predisposition, environmental stressors, early life experiences, and neurobiological factors.

Moreover, distinguishing paranoia from healthy skepticism is critical for understanding its implications. Skepticism, a natural and often beneficial cognitive tool, allows individuals to critically evaluate situations, safeguarding against deception or harm. However, when this skepticism becomes rigid, irrational, or pervasive, it transitions into paranoia, where trust becomes nearly impossible. This shift can lead to social isolation, strained relationships, and a profound sense of alienation.

In this chapter, the core symptoms of paranoia are examined, highlighting how they manifest in daily life and their impact on the individual. The cognitive mechanisms that sustain paranoia, such as hypervigilance, confirmation bias, and emotional reasoning, are explored to reveal how these thought patterns perpetuate the disorder. Additionally, the developmental origins of PPD are traced, focusing on the influence of childhood experiences, attachment styles, and trauma.

The role of genetics and environmental factors is also critical to understanding PPD. Genetic predispositions may increase vulnerability, while environmental stressors, such as unstable or abusive relationships, can trigger or exacerbate paranoid tendencies. Advances in neuroscience have provided insight into how brain structures and functions, such as the overactive amygdala or impaired prefrontal cortex regulation, contribute to the persistence of paranoia.

By distinguishing between healthy skepticism and paranoia, this chapter underscores the importance of context, evidence, and emotional regulation in evaluating threats. While skepticism encourages a balanced and critical approach to potential risks, paranoia leads to a distorted and inflexible view of the world, ultimately compromising one's ability to navigate social and emotional landscapes effectively.

This chapter seeks to demystify paranoia, offering a nuanced perspective that goes beyond stereotypes. By understanding the anatomy of paranoia, both as a symptom and as a disorder, readers can gain insight into the human mind's capacity for both resilience and vulnerability, setting the stage for more compassionate and effective approaches to treatment and support.

Exploring the Core Symptoms of Paranoid Personality Disorder

Paranoid Personality Disorder (PPD) is not merely an amplified form of everyday suspicion or caution. Instead, it represents a pervasive and enduring pattern of distrust and suspicion that significantly affects how individuals perceive, interpret, and engage with the world around them. Unlike the occasional doubts or wariness experienced by most people, PPD alters an individual's core worldview, creating a lens through which every interaction and relationship is scrutinized for potential threats or betrayal. The symptoms of PPD are both cognitive and behavioral, deeply ingrained in the affected person's personality and difficult to manage without intervention.

Persistent Mistrust and Suspicion

The cornerstone of PPD is a profound mistrust of others. Individuals with PPD view the intentions of others as malicious or self-serving, even when evidence points to the contrary. Everyday interactions are filtered through this distorted perception, leading to the misinterpretation of neutral or even kind actions as manipulative or deceitful.

For instance, a coworker's offer to help with a project might be seen as an attempt to undermine one's competence or gain undue credit. Similarly, a neighbor who extends a friendly invitation may be viewed as trying to pry into personal affairs. This pervasive suspicion leaves little room for genuine connections and often isolates the individual socially and emotionally.

This distrust extends even to those closest to them. Family members, close friends, and romantic partners often find their intentions questioned and their actions scrutinized. This dynamic creates a cycle of defensiveness and alienation, with the affected person pushing others away to avoid perceived betrayal while simultaneously lamenting their lack of support or connection.

Preoccupation with Loyalty

An overwhelming concern with loyalty is another defining symptom of PPD. This preoccupation manifests as constant questioning of the fidelity and trustworthiness of others, especially within close relationships. Even trivial actions, such as a delayed response to a message or a casual conversation with someone else, can trigger suspicions of disloyalty or betrayal.

In their quest to confirm loyalty, individuals with PPD may resort to intrusive behaviors. These can include relentless questioning, eavesdropping, or even testing loved ones by creating situations to gauge their reactions. Ironically, these behaviors, aimed at preserving relationships, often have the opposite effect—eroding trust and driving others away.

For example, a person with PPD might accuse a partner of infidelity based on little more than a fleeting glance or an innocent comment. Similarly, a long-time friend who misses a gathering might be seen as harboring hidden resentment or plotting against them. The constant need for reassurance becomes exhausting for both parties, often leading to the breakdown of relationships.

Hostility and Grudge-Holding

Hostility is a frequent companion of PPD, stemming from the individual's tendency to perceive minor slights or disagreements as major offenses. A casual joke, constructive criticism, or an unintentional oversight can be interpreted as a deliberate attack on their character or integrity. These perceived affronts are rarely forgiven or forgotten.

Individuals with PPD are known for holding grudges, sometimes for years, and they may go to great lengths to retaliate against those they believe have wronged them.

This behavior can lead to chronic conflict in their personal and professional lives. For instance, an individual might refuse to attend family gatherings because of a decades-old argument or escalate workplace disagreements to formal grievances.

This hostility often serves as a self-reinforcing mechanism. By responding to perceived threats with anger or defensiveness, they provoke others into actual conflict, which further validates their belief that the world is hostile and untrustworthy.

Reading Hidden Meanings into Events

A hallmark of PPD is the tendency to see hidden, often sinister, meanings in ordinary events or interactions. This symptom reflects a cognitive distortion where neutral or ambiguous situations are interpreted as threatening or deceitful.

For example, a simple compliment from a colleague might be seen as sarcasm or mockery. A manager's decision to assign a new task could be interpreted as an attempt to set them up for failure. These interpretations are not fleeting thoughts but deeply held beliefs that influence how the individual reacts and interacts with others.

This hyper-awareness of perceived slights extends to broader contexts. World events, media messages, or even strangers' actions in public may be interpreted as having personal significance. Such distorted thinking reinforces the individual's sense of being under constant threat, leading to heightened anxiety and defensive behavior.

Emotional Detachment and Guardedness

Emotional detachment is both a symptom and a coping mechanism for individuals with PPD. Their deep-seated mistrust makes it difficult to open up or share personal thoughts and feelings. They fear that any vulnerability might be exploited or used against them.

This guardedness is evident in their interactions and physical demeanor. Many adopt a defensive posture, avoiding eye contact, crossing their arms, or maintaining a rigid stance in social settings. These behaviors signal to others that they are unapproachable or uninterested, further isolating them.

Emotionally, individuals with PPD often appear cold or aloof. They may avoid sharing their joys, fears, or aspirations, even with close friends or family members. This emotional distance creates a barrier to intimacy and understanding, perpetuating the cycle of mistrust and alienation.

The Impact of Core Symptoms

The core symptoms of PPD interact in a way that creates a self-perpetuating cycle of mistrust, defensiveness, and isolation. Persistent suspicion leads to behaviors that alienate others, while the resulting isolation reinforces the individual's belief that the world is untrustworthy. Over time, these patterns can lead to significant impairments in social, occupational, and emotional functioning.

Recognizing and understanding these symptoms is a critical first step in addressing PPD. While the disorder presents significant challenges, it is not insurmountable. With the right combination of therapeutic interventions, support systems, and self-awareness, individuals with PPD can begin to rebuild trust and develop healthier relationships with those around them.

The Cognitive Patterns of Paranoia

The cognitive patterns associated with Paranoid Personality Disorder (PPD) are complex, deeply entrenched, and self-reinforcing. They create a mental framework through which individuals interpret the world, perpetuating cycles of suspicion, misinterpretation, and mistrust. Unlike fleeting moments of doubt or defensiveness, these cognitive distortions are consistent and pervasive, influencing how individuals with PPD process information and interact with others. Understanding these thought patterns sheds light on the mechanisms behind paranoia and offers a foundation for developing strategies to challenge and modify them.

Hypervigilance

Hypervigilance is one of the most defining cognitive features of PPD. People with the disorder remain in a constant state of heightened awareness, scanning their environment for any signs of danger, deceit, or betrayal. This relentless focus on potential threats often stems from a core belief that the world is inherently dangerous and others cannot be trusted.

While hypervigilance can occasionally lead to accurate perceptions of risk, it is frequently a source of misunderstanding and anxiety. The individual's heightened awareness amplifies ordinary, benign cues into signals of potential harm. For instance, an offhand comment in a meeting might be interpreted as a covert insult, or a casual glance from a stranger may be seen as a threatening stare.

This vigilance is exhausting, both mentally and emotionally. It keeps the person in a near-constant state of fight-or-flight, which can erode their ability to focus on other aspects of life, such as work, relationships, or personal well-being. Hypervigilance also fuels confirmation bias, a cognitive distortion that reinforces paranoid beliefs. When someone is always looking for evidence of danger, they are more likely to find—or misinterpret—information that aligns with their fears while dismissing or overlooking evidence to the contrary.

Overgeneralization

Another prominent cognitive distortion in PPD is overgeneralization. This involves taking a single event or interaction and applying its negative implications broadly across situations, people, or time. For example, if a colleague forgets to invite them to a team lunch, the individual might conclude that none of their coworkers respect them or that the entire workplace is hostile.

Overgeneralization reinforces the sense of mistrust and alienation characteristic of PPD. By forming sweeping negative conclusions based on limited evidence, individuals with PPD create mental shortcuts that simplify the complexity of human behavior but lead to inaccurate perceptions. This pattern not only perpetuates their suspicion but also isolates them socially, as they come to view larger groups or categories of people as untrustworthy.

Projection

Projection is another cognitive distortion commonly observed in individuals with PPD. This mechanism involves attributing one's own thoughts, feelings, or motives to others. For someone with PPD, feelings of hostility or mistrust are often unconsciously projected onto those around them. For example, if the individual harbors feelings of resentment or suspicion, they may assume that others feel the same way about them, even in the absence of evidence.

Projection can escalate interpersonal conflicts. Believing that others have negative intentions, the individual with PPD may act defensively or aggressively, provoking responses that appear to confirm their suspicions. This creates a feedback loop where their own actions elicit behaviors in others that reinforce their paranoid worldview.

All-or-Nothing Thinking

Black-and-white thinking, also known as all-or-nothing thinking, is another cognitive hallmark of PPD. This pattern involves viewing situations, people, or relationships in extreme terms, without recognizing nuance or shades of gray. Relationships are categorized as either entirely trustworthy or completely unreliable; events are either good or disastrous; and people are either allies or enemies.

This rigidity makes it difficult for individuals with PPD to maintain relationships or navigate conflicts. A minor disagreement or perceived slight can lead them to completely reevaluate their opinion of someone, shifting from trust to hostility almost instantaneously. For example, a friend's failure to return a phone call might lead to the conclusion that the friend is now untrustworthy or harbors ill intentions, even if the delay is due to something benign, such as being busy.

All-or-nothing thinking prevents reconciliation and growth. Once someone is categorized as "bad" or "untrustworthy," it becomes almost impossible for the individual with PPD to reconsider or revise that judgment, even in the face of new evidence. This rigidity further isolates them, as they struggle to sustain the flexibility and forgiveness necessary for healthy interpersonal relationships.

The Self-Perpetuating Cycle of Cognitive Distortions

The cognitive patterns of PPD do not exist in isolation—they interact to create a self-perpetuating cycle. Hypervigilance leads to confirmation bias, reinforcing overgeneralized conclusions about the untrustworthiness of others. Projection escalates conflicts, making the individual feel more justified in their mistrust. All-or-nothing thinking solidifies these beliefs, making it difficult to break out of the cycle.

For example, consider a scenario where an individual with PPD believes a coworker is conspiring against them. Their hypervigilance causes them to scrutinize every interaction, and confirmation bias ensures they focus only on the coworker's occasional curt responses while ignoring friendly gestures. Overgeneralization leads them to conclude that the entire team is colluding. Projection escalates the situation, as they assume the coworker's neutral expression hides malicious intent, prompting defensive or accusatory behavior that strains the relationship further.

Breaking the Cycle

Understanding these cognitive patterns is a critical step toward breaking the cycle of paranoia. Therapeutic interventions, such as cognitive-behavioral therapy (CBT), can help individuals with PPD identify and challenge their distortions. By recognizing hypervigilance, addressing overgeneralization, confronting projection, and reframing all-or-nothing thinking, individuals can begin to develop healthier and more balanced thought patterns.

While these patterns are deeply ingrained and resistant to change, they are not immutable. With consistent effort and support, it is possible to disrupt the cognitive distortions that fuel PPD, creating space for trust, understanding, and meaningful connections to flourish.

Through this process, individuals can regain a sense of control over their thoughts and emotions, moving toward a more balanced and fulfilling life.

How Paranoia Develops in the Mind

The development of paranoia, particularly as seen in Paranoid Personality Disorder (PPD), is a complex interplay of early experiences, psychological frameworks, and external influences. It is not merely a sudden onset of irrational suspicion but rather a gradual, layered process where certain factors converge to shape a person's view of the world. These elements interact in ways that intensify mistrust and suspicion, embedding paranoia deeply within the individual's cognition and behavior.

Early Life Experiences

Childhood is a critical period during which individuals form foundational beliefs about themselves, others, and the world. In cases of paranoia, early life experiences often lay the groundwork for a mistrustful worldview.

- **Trauma and Neglect:** Traumatic experiences such as physical abuse, emotional neglect, or inconsistent caregiving can lead a child to see relationships as unpredictable or unsafe. For instance, a child who is repeatedly let down by a caregiver might learn to anticipate betrayal or harm as a form of emotional self-defense.

- **Exposure to Conflict:** Growing up in a household marked by frequent arguments, manipulation, or betrayal can also contribute to paranoid thinking. Witnessing parental infidelity or experiencing favoritism among siblings may instill the belief that close relationships are inherently risky.

- **Emotional Unavailability:** When caregivers are emotionally distant or unreliable, a child may feel unsupported and develop a fear of rejection or abandonment. This fear can evolve into a persistent mistrust of others, as the individual struggles to reconcile unmet emotional needs.

Attachment Styles and Their Impact

Attachment theory provides valuable insights into how paranoia develops. The way individuals bond with their primary caregivers in childhood influences their patterns of relating to others throughout life.

- **Insecure Attachment:** Many individuals with PPD display signs of insecure attachment, particularly the anxious or avoidant subtypes. Anxiously attached individuals may fear abandonment, leading to hypervigilance and an overinterpretation of others' actions. Conversely, avoidantly attached individuals may withdraw and distrust others, viewing emotional closeness as a threat.

- **Fear of Betrayal:** Those with insecure attachments often internalize the belief that relationships are unreliable. This fear of betrayal becomes a lens through which they interpret social interactions, heightening the risk of developing paranoia.
- **Difficulty with Trust:** Secure attachment is built on consistent care and mutual trust. Without this foundation, individuals may struggle to trust even when faced with evidence of reliability or goodwill, reinforcing a cycle of suspicion and self-isolation.

The Role of Trauma

Trauma is a significant factor in the development of paranoia. Both acute and chronic trauma can have lasting effects on the brain and psyche, shaping the way individuals perceive and respond to the world.

- **Post-Traumatic Stress Responses:** Traumatic events, such as bullying, discrimination, or violence, can result in heightened arousal states commonly associated with post-traumatic stress disorder (PTSD). These states, characterized by hypervigilance and heightened threat perception, often overlap with the symptoms of paranoia.

- **Avoidance as Protection:** For some, paranoia serves as a protective mechanism to prevent further harm. By assuming the worst in others, individuals believe they are shielding themselves from potential betrayal or danger. While this strategy may feel like self-preservation, it often leads to isolation and an inability to form trusting relationships.

- **Learned Fear:** Repeated exposure to harmful situations can teach individuals to associate people or social interactions with risk. Over time, this learned fear becomes ingrained, making it difficult to distinguish real threats from imagined ones.

Cultural and Social Influences

Paranoia does not exist in a vacuum; cultural and societal factors significantly shape its development. The broader environment in which an individual lives plays a role in reinforcing or challenging paranoid beliefs.

- **Living in High-Stress Environments:** Individuals living in communities marked by systemic injustice, corruption, or high crime rates may develop heightened suspicion as a survival strategy. For example, in regions where government institutions are perceived as untrustworthy, skepticism toward authority may extend to interpersonal relationships.

- **Experiences of Marginalization:** Social exclusion or discrimination based on race, ethnicity, gender, or socioeconomic status can also contribute to paranoia. Repeated experiences of being judged, excluded, or mistreated can lead individuals to develop defensive thought patterns.

- **Media and Misinformation:** Exposure to sensationalist media or conspiracy theories can exacerbate paranoid thinking. The constant portrayal of danger and betrayal in the media can validate preexisting fears, reinforcing a belief that the world is hostile and untrustworthy.

The Cognitive and Emotional Process of Paranoia

Paranoia is not just about external influences; it also involves specific cognitive and emotional processes that evolve over time.

- **Cognitive Distortions:** Cognitive distortions, such as confirmation bias and catastrophizing, play a key role in paranoia's development. These thought patterns encourage individuals to selectively focus on negative or ambiguous stimuli, reinforcing their mistrustful worldview.

- **Emotional Dysregulation:** Heightened emotional sensitivity, particularly to rejection or criticism, can intensify paranoid tendencies. For example, feeling slighted by a colleague might provoke an outsized emotional response, fueling beliefs of malice or conspiracy.
- **Isolation as a Feedback Loop:** Many individuals with PPD isolate themselves to avoid perceived threats. However, this isolation often deprives them of opportunities to challenge their fears or experience positive social interactions, creating a self-reinforcing cycle.

Genetic and Neurological Underpinnings

While environmental and psychological factors are crucial, genetic and biological components also play a role in the development of paranoia.

- **Genetic Vulnerability:** Research suggests that certain genetic predispositions may increase an individual's susceptibility to paranoia. For example, family history of personality disorders or mental health conditions like schizophrenia can be a contributing factor.
- **Neurological Differences:** Paranoia is associated with heightened activity in brain regions responsible for threat detection, such as the amygdala. Overactivity in these areas can

amplify perceptions of danger and reinforce paranoid thinking.

The development of paranoia is a multifaceted process shaped by a combination of early life experiences, attachment styles, trauma, cultural influences, and biological factors. These elements interact to create a worldview dominated by mistrust and suspicion, ultimately manifesting in the pervasive patterns seen in Paranoid Personality Disorder. Recognizing the underlying factors that contribute to paranoia's development is essential for providing effective interventions and fostering understanding. By addressing the roots of paranoia, individuals can begin to break free from its grip and move toward healthier, more trusting relationships.

The Role of Genetics and Environment

Paranoid Personality Disorder (PPD) does not arise in isolation. Its roots lie in a complex interplay between genetic predispositions and environmental influences, shaping how individuals perceive and respond to the world. Understanding this interaction offers valuable insights into the disorder's development, revealing how inherited vulnerabilities and life experiences intertwine to create the enduring patterns of mistrust and suspicion characteristic of PPD.

Genetic Factors

A growing body of research points to a genetic component in the development of PPD. Studies on familial patterns have shown that individuals with a family history of personality disorders, particularly Cluster A disorders such as schizotypal or schizoid personality disorder, or schizophrenia, have an increased likelihood of developing PPD. These findings suggest that genetic predispositions may lay the groundwork for the cognitive and emotional vulnerabilities seen in paranoia.

Genetic contributions to PPD are believed to influence brain structures and functions that regulate emotions and process threats. For instance, variations in genes associated with dopamine and serotonin pathways may affect emotional regulation, social processing, and the ability to differentiate between genuine and perceived threats. Such differences might predispose individuals to heightened sensitivity to social cues, making them more susceptible to interpreting benign interactions as hostile or deceitful.

Neurobiological Contributions

Advances in neuroimaging have shed light on the biological underpinnings of paranoia. Studies reveal that individuals with PPD often exhibit heightened activity in the amygdala, a brain region responsible for processing fear and detecting threats. This overactivity may explain their tendency to perceive danger even in safe environments.

Other studies have identified dysregulation in the prefrontal cortex, which plays a role in decision-making and emotional regulation. Reduced connectivity between the prefrontal cortex and the amygdala may impair an individual's ability to modulate emotional responses, making it harder to override fear-driven interpretations of social interactions. Together, these neurobiological factors contribute to the pervasive mistrust and defensiveness observed in PPD.

Environmental Triggers

While genetics and neurobiology provide the foundation, environmental factors play a pivotal role in shaping the expression of PPD. Early-life experiences, particularly those involving trauma, neglect, or chronic stress, are significant contributors.

Trauma and Betrayal

Traumatic events, especially those involving betrayal or exploitation by trusted individuals, can leave deep psychological scars. These experiences may prime the individual to expect harm or deceit in future relationships, reinforcing paranoid thought patterns. For example, a child who grows up in an environment where caregivers are unreliable or abusive may develop hypervigilance as a survival mechanism, which can later evolve into the pervasive mistrust characteristic of PPD.

Chronic Stress

Prolonged exposure to stressful environments can also exacerbate paranoid tendencies. Living in situations where mistrust is justified—such as in abusive relationships, unsafe neighborhoods, or workplaces with toxic dynamics—can validate and intensify an individual's suspicion of others. Over time, this mistrust may become generalized, extending beyond the specific environment to all aspects of the person's life.

Parenting Styles and Family Dynamics

Certain parenting styles and family dynamics have been linked to the development of PPD. Overly controlling, critical, or emotionally distant parenting can contribute to feelings of inadequacy and insecurity. These feelings may manifest as defensiveness and hypersensitivity to perceived threats later in life. Similarly, growing up in a family with high levels of conflict, secrecy, or distrust can normalize paranoid attitudes, shaping the child's worldview and interpersonal expectations.

Epigenetics and PPD

The emerging field of epigenetics offers new perspectives on how environmental factors interact with genetic predispositions to influence the development of PPD. Epigenetics refers to changes in gene expression caused by environmental influences, without altering the underlying DNA sequence.

Stress and Gene Expression
Chronic stress or trauma, particularly during critical periods of brain development, can alter the expression of genes related to the stress response and emotional regulation. For instance, prolonged exposure to adversity may increase the sensitivity of the hypothalamic-pituitary-adrenal (HPA) axis, the body's central stress-response system. This heightened sensitivity can make individuals more reactive to perceived threats, reinforcing the cognitive distortions associated with paranoia.

Intergenerational Transmission
Epigenetic changes may also be passed down through generations, contributing to familial patterns of PPD. For example, a parent who has experienced trauma may develop coping mechanisms or behavioral patterns rooted in mistrust, which are then modeled for and adopted by their children. Additionally, epigenetic markers shaped by the parent's experiences can

influence the child's stress response systems, increasing their susceptibility to developing PPD under certain environmental conditions.

The Interplay of Nature and Nurture

PPD cannot be fully attributed to either genetic or environmental factors alone; rather, it is the product of their interaction. Genetic predispositions may create vulnerabilities, but these only translate into PPD when activated or exacerbated by environmental triggers. Conversely, even individuals without a strong genetic predisposition can develop PPD if exposed to severe or prolonged environmental stressors.

For example, consider a person with a family history of personality disorders and heightened amygdala activity. If this individual grows up in a stable, supportive environment, their genetic predispositions may never manifest as PPD. However, if they experience chronic abuse or betrayal, these vulnerabilities may be activated, leading to the development of paranoid thought patterns.

Pathways to Prevention and Intervention

Understanding the role of genetics and environment in PPD opens the door to targeted prevention and intervention strategies. For individuals with a known genetic predisposition, early-life interventions focused on building trust, resilience, and emotional regulation can mitigate the risk of developing PPD.

Trauma-informed care and therapeutic approaches, such as cognitive-behavioral therapy (CBT) or dialectical behavior therapy (DBT), can help individuals process past experiences and challenge distorted thought patterns. On a broader scale, creating safe, supportive environments—both within families and communities—can reduce the environmental stressors that contribute to PPD.

By addressing both the biological and environmental factors that shape PPD, it is possible to break the cycle of paranoia, paving the way for healthier thought patterns and relationships. The interplay between genetics and environment highlights the dynamic nature of PPD and underscores the importance of a holistic approach to understanding and treating the disorder.

Key Differences Between Healthy Skepticism and Paranoia

At first glance, healthy skepticism and paranoia might seem to exist on the same continuum of doubt and caution. Both involve questioning the motives and actions of others, particularly in uncertain or ambiguous situations. However, the similarities end there. Healthy skepticism is a rational, adaptive approach to navigating the complexities of human interaction and decision-making. Paranoia, in contrast, is irrational, rigid, and often maladaptive, deeply impairing relationships and overall functioning. Understanding the distinctions between these two states of mind is essential for appreciating the dynamics of Paranoid Personality Disorder (PPD).

Basis in Reality

Healthy skepticism is firmly rooted in evidence and reason. It is a thought process that engages critical thinking, weighing facts and experiences to make informed judgments. For instance, a skeptical individual may question the reliability of a sales pitch but seek out verifiable reviews or testimonials before drawing conclusions. Skepticism is a tool for discernment, allowing individuals to protect themselves from harm or deception without dismissing the possibility of good intentions.

Paranoia, however, lacks this grounding in reality. It is characterized by pervasive, unfounded suspicions that persist even when confronted with evidence to the contrary. For example, a person with PPD might interpret a simple greeting as an attempt to mask hostile intentions, holding onto this belief regardless of assurances or behavioral evidence that suggest otherwise. This disconnect from reality is a defining feature of paranoia, making it a significant barrier to healthy relationships and decision-making.

Flexibility of Thought

A critical difference between skepticism and paranoia lies in the ability to adapt. Skepticism is inherently flexible; it allows for the revision of beliefs and assumptions when presented with new or better information. A skeptical person can weigh opposing viewpoints, consider alternative explanations, and adjust their perspective accordingly. This cognitive flexibility is a hallmark of sound reasoning and emotional intelligence.

In contrast, paranoia is marked by cognitive rigidity. Individuals with paranoid tendencies often cling to their suspicions, regardless of how much evidence disproves them. Challenges to their beliefs may even intensify their mistrust, as they perceive such challenges as further proof of deception or hostility. This inflexibility traps individuals in a cycle of suspicion and alienation, preventing growth or reconciliation.

Impact on Relationships

The effect of skepticism and paranoia on relationships is another stark difference. Healthy skepticism can actually enhance relationships by encouraging open communication and fostering mutual understanding. For instance, questioning a partner's motives in a particular situation, when done respectfully, can lead to greater clarity and trust. Skeptical individuals are open to hearing explanations and resolving misunderstandings, strengthening their connections with others.

Paranoia, on the other hand, is corrosive to relationships. Individuals with PPD often assume malicious intent even in neutral or kind gestures, leading to defensiveness, accusations, or withdrawal. They may perceive close friends or family members as betrayers, interpreting innocent actions as signs of conspiracy. Over time, this constant suspicion alienates others, leaving the individual isolated and reinforcing their belief that no one can be trusted.

Emotional Regulation

Healthy skepticism operates within a framework of emotional balance. A skeptical individual may feel mild concern or wariness, but these emotions are proportionate to the situation and do not overwhelm their ability to think clearly. Emotional regulation enables skeptics to approach situations objectively, keeping their responses measured and constructive.

In contrast, paranoia is often accompanied by intense, dysregulated emotions such as fear, anxiety, and anger. These heightened emotions can cloud judgment, amplifying misinterpretations and making it difficult to distinguish between real and imagined threats. For example, a person with paranoia may feel extreme anger at a perceived slight, responding with hostility that escalates the situation unnecessarily. These emotional outbursts further entrench paranoid beliefs, creating a vicious cycle.

Functional vs. Dysfunctional

Ultimately, the most significant difference between healthy skepticism and paranoia is their impact on an individual's functionality. Skepticism is a practical tool that enhances problem-solving, decision-making, and personal growth. It protects against gullibility and exploitation while fostering a balanced approach to uncertainty. Skeptical individuals can navigate complex social and professional environments effectively, building constructive relationships and achieving their goals.

Paranoia, on the other hand, is inherently dysfunctional. It disrupts daily life by fostering mistrust, conflict, and isolation. Paranoid individuals may struggle to maintain relationships, hold down jobs, or engage in social activities, as their perceptions of threat and betrayal overshadow reality. Their hypervigilance and defensive behaviors often lead to unnecessary conflict and emotional exhaustion, further diminishing their quality of life.

Navigating the Boundary

Recognizing the boundary between healthy skepticism and paranoia is crucial, particularly in contexts where trust and discernment are essential. While skepticism encourages inquiry and reflection, paranoia shuts down possibilities, locking individuals into a world of fear and suspicion.

In understanding this distinction, it becomes clear that paranoia, as seen in PPD, is not simply skepticism taken to an extreme. It is a fundamentally different phenomenon, shaped by biological, psychological, and environmental factors that distort perception and impair functioning. By distinguishing paranoia from skepticism, mental health professionals and caregivers can better support individuals with PPD, guiding them toward healthier patterns of thought and interaction.

This understanding also underscores the importance of cultivating emotional intelligence and critical thinking skills in society. Encouraging these traits can help individuals navigate uncertainty with clarity and confidence, reducing the risk of paranoia and fostering stronger, more trusting communities.

Chapter 2: The Science of Paranoia

Paranoia, particularly when it manifests as Paranoid Personality Disorder (PPD), is not simply an exaggerated reaction to external threats or life stressors. It is far more intricate, rooted in the deep workings of the brain, shaped by both genetic predispositions and the environment in which a person develops. This chapter takes a closer look at the neurobiological foundations of PPD, exploring how the brain's functions contribute to the paranoid thought patterns that characterize the disorder. We will also examine how external factors, such as stress and life experiences, play a critical role in amplifying paranoid thoughts. Through a deeper understanding of these biological and environmental influences, we can begin to unravel the complex processes that give rise to paranoia and the ways in which it disrupts daily life.

The brain, a highly adaptive and malleable organ, is the epicenter of both healthy cognitive functions and those that become distorted in PPD. Neurobiological research has shed light on the brain's role in processing fear, trust, and emotional regulation—areas that are central to the experience of paranoia. Overactive brain regions involved in threat detection, alongside altered brain chemistry, help explain why individuals with PPD perceive others as being hostile or deceitful, even when there is little or no evidence to support such conclusions.

Genetic factors also play a critical role in the development of PPD, suggesting that certain inherited traits may predispose an individual to develop paranoid thinking patterns. These genetic predispositions can influence brain structures and the way they respond to stress, fear, and social interaction. However, the influence of genetics is not deterministic—environmental factors such as early trauma, betrayal, or chronic stress also play a crucial part in shaping the severity and expression of paranoia in individuals. Together, the neurobiological and environmental factors create a framework that influences how paranoia develops and persists in those with PPD.

Moreover, the advances in brain imaging techniques, such as functional MRI and PET scans, have made it possible to observe and measure brain activity in real-time. These tools have given scientists the ability to map out the areas of the brain that are most active during paranoid thought processes, offering valuable insights into the underlying mechanisms of PPD. By examining these developments, we gain a clearer understanding of how paranoia operates not only as a psychological phenomenon but as a brain-based disorder that involves complex neural pathways and chemical imbalances.

Ultimately, this chapter aims to provide a comprehensive look at the science of paranoia, offering insights into how the brain's neurobiology and external influences contribute to the development of Paranoid Personality Disorder. Understanding these factors is crucial for developing more effective approaches to diagnosis and treatment, and it opens the door to exploring new therapeutic avenues to help those affected by PPD lead more functional and balanced lives.

Neurobiological Factors Behind PPD

The neurobiology of paranoia, particularly in the context of Paranoid Personality Disorder (PPD), involves a complex interplay of brain structures and chemical systems that contribute to heightened suspicion and distorted perceptions of reality. While research into the neurobiological underpinnings of PPD is ongoing, emerging findings shed light on the brain's threat detection system, which plays a critical role in the disorder's development and persistence.

Central to this system is the amygdala, a small but crucial region of the brain that processes fear and emotional responses. The amygdala is essentially the brain's alarm system, alerting us to potential threats in our environment. In individuals with PPD, studies have shown that this area is often hyperactive, meaning that the brain reacts with an exaggerated sense of threat, even when no actual danger is present. This heightened activity can lead to the misinterpretation of neutral social cues—such as a person's neutral facial expression or a slight delay in responding to a message—as hostile or threatening. As a result, everyday interactions that would be innocuous to most people are viewed through a lens of suspicion and fear, reinforcing the individual's paranoid beliefs.

Dopamine, a neurotransmitter involved in regulating mood, attention, and reward processing, also plays a significant role in paranoia. Research indicates that dysregulation of dopamine, particularly in the mesolimbic pathway, can contribute to the overactivation of the brain's threat-detection circuits. When dopamine levels become imbalanced, the brain may become excessively focused on potential dangers, making it difficult for the individual to assess situations objectively. The constant state of heightened alertness, fueled by an overactive dopamine system, can lead to a persistent belief that others are plotting harm or acting with malicious intent. This imbalance in dopamine processing not only amplifies paranoia but also creates a cycle where the individual is unable to interpret neutral or benign interactions in any other way.

Another key player in the neurobiology of paranoia is the prefrontal cortex, the area of the brain responsible for higher-order cognitive functions such as decision-making, impulse control, and judgment. The prefrontal cortex acts as the brain's regulator, helping to temper emotional responses that may arise from the amygdala. However, in individuals with PPD, research suggests that the prefrontal cortex may not function optimally in regulating the intense emotional reactions produced by the amygdala. This lack of regulation can result in an inability to assess situations with balance and reason, leading to an automatic and disproportionate emotional response to perceived threats. The failure to inhibit exaggerated threat detection further perpetuates feelings of suspicion and mistrust.

In sum, the neurobiological factors behind PPD involve a disruption in the brain's ability to process and regulate fear and threat responses. The overactive amygdala, dopamine dysregulation, and impaired prefrontal cortex functioning all contribute to the cognitive distortions that define paranoia. These neurobiological mechanisms explain why individuals with PPD often find it difficult to trust others and are prone to seeing malice where there is none. Understanding these brain-based factors is essential for developing more effective treatments, as interventions that target these specific systems could help individuals with PPD better manage their paranoia and improve their quality of life.

Brain Function and Paranoid Thought Processes

The brain's functional connectivity plays a significant role in shaping how individuals with Paranoid Personality Disorder (PPD) interpret their experiences and the world around them. Paranoia, at its core, is driven by cognitive distortions—patterns of thinking that consistently lead individuals to misinterpret or overreact to situations. In the case of PPD, these thought patterns are not random but rather the result of how various brain regions communicate and process information. When these networks become dysregulated, paranoid thoughts can take hold, creating a cycle of mistrust and suspicion.

A crucial network involved in paranoid thinking is the default mode network (DMN), a collection of brain regions that are active when we are not focused on external tasks but instead engaged in self-reflection, daydreaming, or mind-wandering. The DMN is often associated with our internal thought processes and, more specifically, with our tendency to ruminate. In individuals with PPD, research suggests that this network can become overactive, leading to a state where the mind is constantly cycling through its thoughts and interpretations of the world. When the DMN is hyperactive, individuals may become excessively focused on their own inner world, leading them to overanalyze even the most mundane events or interactions. A neutral comment from a colleague may be interpreted as a veiled insult, or a minor lapse in communication may be seen as a deliberate slight.

This tendency to overanalyze situations can create a feedback loop, where the individual's suspicions only increase in intensity as they mentally replay and scrutinize their interactions. The more they focus on these perceived slights or hidden motives, the more convinced they become that others are acting with malicious intent. This constant rumination prevents individuals with PPD from finding resolution or understanding in their relationships, pushing them further into isolation and reinforcing their feelings of mistrust. The DMN's overactivity may make it difficult for them to break free from this cycle of negative thinking, keeping them locked in a distorted worldview.

Another brain structure that plays a crucial role in regulating emotional responses and thought processes is the anterior cingulate cortex (ACC). The ACC is involved in monitoring emotional reactions, recognizing when emotions become disproportionate, and adjusting responses accordingly. It also helps individuals resolve conflicts and navigate social situations by providing a sense of emotional balance and insight into how one's actions or thoughts may affect others. However, in individuals with PPD, the ACC may not function as effectively as it should. This dysfunction can lead to a heightened sensitivity to perceived slights or social rejection, causing individuals to overreact emotionally when they feel criticized or ignored.

Normally, the ACC helps us regulate our emotions and adjust our responses when we realize that we are misinterpreting a situation. For example, if we feel slighted by a comment, the ACC would guide us to consider alternative explanations, such as the possibility that the comment was not intended to hurt us. In individuals with PPD, however, the ACC may fail to provide this kind of emotional regulation, causing the person to interpret every interaction through a lens of suspicion and defensiveness. This failure to moderate emotional reactions can fuel the distorted thinking patterns that characterize paranoia, as the individual becomes more entrenched in their negative beliefs about others.

Together, the overactivity of the DMN and the impaired function of the ACC create a potent combination that drives the cognitive distortions seen in PPD. The brain becomes stuck in a cycle of rumination, emotional overreaction, and misinterpretation of social cues, reinforcing feelings of mistrust and alienation. These brain-based mechanisms help explain why individuals with PPD are so prone to suspicion and why they find it difficult to break free from their paranoid thoughts. Understanding these processes provides insight into the complexity of the disorder and underscores the importance of targeted interventions that address both the brain's functioning and the thought patterns that underlie paranoia.

The Role of Stress in Paranoia

Stress plays a crucial role in both triggering and intensifying paranoid thoughts in individuals with Paranoid Personality Disorder (PPD). When a person with PPD experiences stress, it can create a physiological and psychological response that amplifies their feelings of mistrust and suspicion. This response is not just a temporary reaction—it can lead to long-lasting changes in brain function and thought patterns that perpetuate paranoia.

One of the primary ways that stress influences paranoia is through the body's stress response system, specifically the release of cortisol. Cortisol is a hormone that is released during times of stress and is often referred to as the "stress hormone." While cortisol plays a vital role in helping the body respond to immediate threats, prolonged or chronic stress can have harmful effects, particularly on brain regions involved in emotional regulation and threat detection. The amygdala, which is responsible for processing fear and detecting threats, becomes more sensitive under high cortisol levels. This heightened sensitivity means that individuals with PPD are more likely to perceive neutral or innocuous social interactions as threats. For example, a simple comment from a coworker might be interpreted as an insult or a sign of betrayal, leading to an emotional overreaction.

Additionally, chronic stress can impair the hippocampus, a region of the brain involved in memory processing and emotional regulation. The hippocampus helps individuals distinguish between past and present experiences, allowing them to contextualize current events based on previous knowledge and memories. When the hippocampus is impaired, individuals may struggle to differentiate between real and perceived threats. Past betrayals or emotional wounds can become intertwined with present situations, causing the individual to interpret new interactions as hostile, even when there is no basis for such an interpretation.

The impact of stress extends beyond just biological changes—it also influences how individuals with PPD interact with others. Stress increases feelings of vulnerability, making it even harder for them to trust those around them. This heightened anxiety can lead to a pattern of overreaction in social situations, where the individual sees slights or attacks even when none exist. As a result, they may become increasingly withdrawn, defensive, or combative, which further isolates them from others. This cycle of stress, mistrust, and social withdrawal can create a barrier to seeking help or engaging in therapeutic interventions, reinforcing the paranoid thought patterns that underlie the disorder.

Furthermore, individuals with PPD may already have a heightened sensitivity to perceived betrayal or rejection, and stress only exacerbates these tendencies. In stressful situations, the brain's threat detection system becomes hyperactive, causing individuals to overanalyze interactions and misinterpret the motives of others. Even well-meaning actions or neutral behaviors can be seen as deliberate attempts to deceive or undermine them.

The relationship between stress and paranoia highlights the complexity of PPD. Stress not only worsens paranoid thoughts but also limits the individual's ability to engage in healthy social connections and seek support. Understanding the role of stress in the development and maintenance of paranoia is crucial for developing effective treatment strategies. Interventions aimed at managing stress and promoting emotional regulation can help individuals with PPD break the cycle of suspicion and isolation, leading to improved functioning and quality of life.

Advances in Brain Imaging Studies

Recent advancements in brain imaging technologies have provided groundbreaking insights into the brain activity of individuals with Paranoid Personality Disorder (PPD), allowing researchers to gain a deeper understanding of the neurobiological underpinnings of paranoia. Techniques such as functional magnetic resonance imaging (fMRI) and positron emission tomography (PET) scans have made it possible to observe real-time brain function and identify specific patterns of activity that are associated with paranoid thought processes.

fMRI studies have highlighted some of the key brain regions involved in PPD. One of the most consistent findings is the heightened activity in the amygdala, a brain structure that plays a central role in processing fear and detecting threats. When individuals with PPD are exposed to social or emotional stimuli, their amygdala tends to become overly active, suggesting an exaggerated threat detection system. This overactivity may explain why individuals with PPD interpret neutral or even benign social cues as dangerous, fueling their chronic suspicion and mistrust.

On the other hand, areas of the brain involved in higher cognitive functions, such as the prefrontal cortex, show reduced activation in individuals with PPD. The prefrontal cortex is responsible for regulating emotional responses, making decisions, and controlling impulses. The decreased activation in this region indicates that individuals with PPD may struggle to control their emotional reactions to perceived threats, leading to a heightened sense of fear and difficulty distinguishing between real and imagined dangers. This imbalance between the emotional regions (like the amygdala) and the cognitive-regulatory areas (like the prefrontal cortex) could explain why individuals with PPD experience such intense emotional reactions and distorted perceptions.

PET scans have also contributed valuable information, particularly in regard to neurotransmitter activity. Dopamine, a neurotransmitter involved in mood regulation, reward processing, and attention, plays a critical role in the development of paranoid thoughts. Studies using PET scans have shown that individuals with PPD may exhibit altered dopamine receptor activity in certain brain regions, suggesting that dopamine dysregulation is involved in the formation and maintenance of paranoid ideation. This dysregulation could cause individuals to perceive threats where none exist and reinforce the belief that others are untrustworthy or hostile.

These advances in brain imaging have provided a more precise model of how paranoia manifests in the brain. By identifying the specific neural circuits and neurotransmitter systems involved, researchers have been able to develop a better understanding of the biological mechanisms that contribute to paranoid thinking. This knowledge has opened up new possibilities for targeted treatments, such as interventions that aim to regulate dopamine levels or enhance prefrontal cortex function, in order to help individuals with PPD manage their paranoia and improve their quality of life.

As brain imaging technology continues to evolve, it holds the potential to further refine our understanding of PPD and other mental health conditions. By examining the brain activity associated with various cognitive and emotional processes, scientists can develop more effective, individualized treatments for those struggling with paranoia. This research also offers hope for the development of early detection methods and more personalized interventions, ultimately improving outcomes for individuals with PPD and related disorders.

The Influence of Genetics in Paranoid Personality Development

Genetics plays a significant role in the development of Paranoid Personality Disorder (PPD), influencing how the brain processes social information and responds to perceived threats. While environmental factors, such as trauma, abuse, or betrayal, often act as triggers for paranoia, research indicates that genetic predispositions are key contributors to the disorder's onset and progression.

A wealth of evidence suggests that individuals with a family history of personality disorders, especially those characterized by distrust, aggression, or antisocial behavior, are at a higher risk of developing PPD. This pattern of inheritance implies that certain genetic factors related to emotional regulation, threat detection, and social processing may predispose individuals to develop paranoid traits. These genetic components can affect how individuals perceive and respond to social interactions, making them more likely to misinterpret neutral or benign behavior as threatening or malicious.

Researchers have pinpointed specific genes that are involved in the regulation of neurotransmitters such as serotonin and dopamine. Both serotonin and dopamine play a critical role in mood regulation, emotional processing, and social behavior. Dysregulation in these neurotransmitter systems has been implicated in a range of personality disorders, including PPD. The imbalance in serotonin levels, for instance, may affect mood stability, while abnormalities in dopamine function are thought to influence the brain's reward system and the perception of threat. These neurotransmitter imbalances may contribute to the distorted perceptions and heightened vigilance characteristic of paranoia.

Twin studies have further solidified the genetic connection to PPD, showing that individuals who share genetic material with someone diagnosed with the disorder are more likely to exhibit similar personality traits. These studies highlight the heritable nature of paranoid thinking, although they also emphasize that genetics alone do not determine whether someone will develop PPD. Instead, genetic predispositions interact with environmental influences, such as childhood experiences, to shape the development of paranoid traits.

This interaction between genes and environment is also explored through the lens of epigenetics. Epigenetics refers to the way environmental factors can influence gene expression without altering the underlying DNA sequence. Traumatic events, particularly those experienced during formative years, can trigger epigenetic changes that affect how genes involved in stress response and emotional regulation are expressed. For example, early exposure to chronic stress or abuse may lead to alterations in the expression of genes related to the body's stress response, making individuals more susceptible to developing paranoia. These epigenetic changes may also increase the likelihood of psychiatric disorders later in life, compounding the individual's vulnerability to paranoia.

In conclusion, the development of Paranoid Personality Disorder is the result of a complex interplay between genetics, neurobiology, and environmental factors. Genetic predispositions contribute to the brain's sensitivity to threat, emotional regulation, and social processing, while environmental experiences, particularly trauma or abuse, can activate or exacerbate these tendencies. Furthermore, epigenetic mechanisms provide insight into how life experiences can influence the expression of genes and contribute to the development of paranoid traits. By understanding the genetic, neurobiological, and environmental influences that shape PPD, clinicians and researchers are better equipped to address the challenges of diagnosing and treating this complex disorder. Advances in brain imaging and research into the molecular underpinnings of paranoia offer promising avenues for more effective interventions, ultimately improving the quality of life for those affected by PPD.

Chapter 3: Unpacking the Causes and Triggers

Paranoid Personality Disorder (PPD) emerges from a complex interplay of various influences, combining a person's genetic predisposition, early life experiences, environmental exposures, and cultural factors. It is not simply the result of one isolated cause but rather the culmination of diverse elements interacting over time. This chapter explores these interconnected factors, shedding light on how childhood experiences, trauma, family dynamics, societal influences, and substance use contribute to the development and persistence of PPD. By examining these underlying causes and triggers, we can better understand how paranoia is shaped and sustained, paving the way for more effective approaches to treatment and support.

Early experiences, such as inconsistent caregiving or exposure to bullying, lay the groundwork for mistrust and suspicion, which can evolve into a rigid worldview. Traumatic events and chronic stressors amplify these patterns, teaching individuals to anticipate danger even in safe circumstances. Family dynamics, including overbearing parenting or betrayal within close relationships, further reinforce paranoid tendencies, while cultural norms and historical injustices shape how paranoia is expressed and interpreted. Additionally, substance use can exacerbate paranoia, altering brain chemistry and magnifying feelings of suspicion and fear.

Each of these influences plays a significant role in molding the paranoid mindset, often creating a self-perpetuating cycle that deepens mistrust and isolates the individual. Understanding these multifaceted contributors not only helps in diagnosing and treating PPD but also highlights the importance of addressing the broader context in which the disorder arises.

Childhood Experiences and Their Influence on Paranoia

Childhood lays the foundation for how individuals perceive the world and others within it. For those who develop Paranoid Personality Disorder (PPD), early experiences often foster deep-seated mistrust and a heightened sense of vulnerability. The influence of attachment issues, negative peer interactions, and exposure to instability plays a significant role in shaping the paranoid mindset that defines PPD.

The Role of Attachment Issues

Attachment theory underscores the importance of stable, nurturing relationships in early childhood for developing trust and emotional security. When children receive consistent care, they learn to rely on others and perceive the world as a generally safe place. However, when caregiving is inconsistent, neglectful, or abusive, a child's ability to trust can be severely impaired.

Children who grow up in emotionally neglectful environments may internalize the belief that they cannot depend on others. For instance, emotionally unavailable parents might unintentionally teach their children that seeking support from others is futile. This can lead to excessive self-reliance, a characteristic often observed in individuals with PPD. Over time, this self-reliance transforms into suspicion, as the individual becomes hypervigilant, interpreting others' actions as potential threats to their autonomy or safety.

Bullying and Peer Rejection

Interactions with peers during formative years significantly influence social development. Experiences of bullying, ridicule, or exclusion during childhood and adolescence can leave lasting psychological scars. For a child who is frequently marginalized, the repeated emotional wounds foster a view of the world as hostile.

A child subjected to bullying may begin to perceive even neutral or friendly interactions with suspicion, fearing hidden motives or ridicule. For instance, a compliment from a peer might be interpreted as sarcasm or mockery. When such patterns of thinking become entrenched, they often persist into adulthood, forming the cognitive underpinnings of PPD. In adulthood, these individuals may struggle to differentiate between genuine interactions and perceived threats, viewing most relationships with guarded skepticism.

Exposure to Unpredictable Environments

Growing up in an environment marked by unpredictability and chaos—such as a household affected by domestic violence, parental conflict, or substance abuse—can have profound effects on a child's emotional development. In such circumstances, children are often forced to remain on high alert, anticipating potential danger as a means of survival.

This heightened state of vigilance, while adaptive in a volatile environment, can become maladaptive later in life when the individual is in safer, more stable circumstances. A person raised in an unpredictable home may develop a constant need to anticipate the worst, mistrusting others' intentions even in benign situations. For example, a person who grew up in a household where arguments often escalated into violence might interpret a raised voice as a precursor to aggression, even in a calm or professional setting.

Fear of Betrayal and Emotional Vulnerability

Childhood betrayals, whether from a caregiver, teacher, or trusted adult, can leave lasting impressions on how trust is formed and maintained. Instances of broken promises or violations of trust can plant the seeds of paranoia. A child who feels betrayed may develop a protective mechanism of expecting the worst from others to avoid future disappointment or harm.

In some cases, betrayal leads to a rigid belief that others are inherently deceptive or self-serving. This belief often becomes self-reinforcing: the individual's guardedness and suspicion can provoke defensiveness or withdrawal from others, which in turn appears to validate their mistrust.

The Intergenerational Transmission of Paranoia

Paranoia can also be indirectly passed down through family dynamics. Parents or caregivers who display paranoid tendencies themselves may model behaviors and attitudes that shape their children's worldview. A child raised in a household where mistrust is pervasive—such as one where parents frequently accuse neighbors, friends, or family members of ill intent—may internalize these paranoid attitudes as normal.

Additionally, family environments marked by excessive criticism, punishment, or unrealistic expectations can instill a fear of being judged or betrayed. For example, a child whose achievements are never acknowledged but whose mistakes are harshly punished may grow into an adult who anticipates scrutiny or exploitation in every interaction.

Long-Term Impacts of Childhood Experiences

The psychological effects of early experiences often persist well into adulthood, shaping an individual's emotional responses, cognitive processes, and interpersonal behaviors. For individuals predisposed to PPD, these experiences create a lens of suspicion and self-protection that colors all aspects of life. The inability to process childhood wounds in a healthy way can lead to a chronic state of defensiveness, preventing the development of meaningful and trusting relationships.

By understanding the role of childhood experiences in the development of paranoia, mental health professionals and caregivers can better identify early warning signs and provide timely interventions. Building emotional resilience and fostering secure attachments in childhood can serve as protective factors, potentially mitigating the risk of PPD in later life.

Trauma and Stress: Key Catalysts for PPD

Trauma and prolonged stress are significant factors in the development and progression of Paranoid Personality Disorder (PPD). These experiences often serve as catalysts, either amplifying inherent vulnerabilities or creating new psychological pathways that foster distrust and hypervigilance. By understanding the mechanisms through which trauma and chronic stress shape paranoia, we can better appreciate their profound impact on the psyche.

Acute Trauma and Its Aftermath

A single traumatic event can drastically alter an individual's sense of safety and trust. Events such as physical assault, betrayal by a trusted individual, or surviving a life-threatening situation leave psychological imprints that are difficult to erase. These experiences often lead to hyperarousal, a state in which the mind remains in constant anticipation of danger. Even in secure environments, individuals affected by trauma may struggle to feel safe, interpreting neutral situations as threatening.

For example, someone who has been betrayed by a close friend may become wary of others, questioning their motives and sincerity. This heightened suspicion, initially a defense mechanism to avoid further harm, can become ingrained over time, forming the basis for paranoid thinking. The inability to distinguish between genuine threats and benign interactions is a hallmark of paranoia and a common consequence of unresolved trauma.

Chronic Stress and Its Impact on Cognition

While acute trauma creates immediate disruption, chronic stress exerts a more gradual but equally damaging effect. Persistent exposure to stressful environments, such as unsafe neighborhoods, toxic workplaces, or abusive relationships, forces the brain to operate in survival mode for extended periods. This ongoing activation of the stress response system floods the brain with cortisol, a hormone associated with the fight-or-flight response.

Elevated cortisol levels over time impair emotional regulation and cognitive processing, making it harder to evaluate situations objectively. This hormonal imbalance can lead to exaggerated interpretations of others' actions, reinforcing patterns of mistrust. For individuals with a predisposition to PPD, chronic stress solidifies these thought patterns, blurring the line between genuine and perceived threats.

For instance, someone enduring workplace harassment may begin to suspect that not only their harasser but also neutral colleagues are conspiring against them. This generalization of mistrust exacerbates feelings of isolation and perpetuates paranoid behaviors.

The Role of Complex Trauma

Complex Post-Traumatic Stress Disorder (C-PTSD), a condition stemming from prolonged or repeated trauma, often overlaps with the symptoms of PPD. Both conditions share features such as hypervigilance, emotional dysregulation, and difficulty forming trusting relationships. However, the relationship between these conditions is nuanced.

For individuals with C-PTSD, paranoia can emerge as a coping mechanism, providing a sense of control in environments perceived as hostile or unpredictable. The mind, conditioned by repeated exposure to harm, becomes adept at identifying potential threats—sometimes to the point of seeing danger where none exists. This hyperawareness, while protective in traumatic settings, becomes maladaptive in everyday life, fostering unnecessary suspicion and conflict.

Trauma's Role in Shaping Worldview

Trauma not only affects an individual's emotional state but also reshapes their worldview. Someone who has experienced significant trauma may adopt a belief system in which trust is seen as dangerous, vulnerability as weakness, and others as inherently deceitful. These beliefs become self-reinforcing over time, as the individual selectively focuses on interactions that confirm their fears while disregarding evidence to the contrary.

For example, if a person with PPD perceives rejection from a friend, this experience may validate their preexisting belief that others are unreliable or malicious. These patterns, deeply rooted in trauma, make it challenging to break the cycle of paranoia without targeted intervention.

The Self-Perpetuating Cycle of Stress and Paranoia

One of the most damaging effects of trauma and stress in PPD is the creation of a self-perpetuating cycle. The more an individual experiences fear and mistrust, the more likely they are to behave in ways that alienate others, such as being overly defensive or accusatory. This, in turn, elicits negative reactions from others, which seem to confirm the individual's suspicions. Over time, this cycle isolates the person further, leaving them trapped in their paranoid beliefs.

Pathways to Healing

Understanding the role of trauma and stress in the development of PPD highlights the importance of early intervention and support. Trauma-focused therapies, such as cognitive-behavioral therapy (CBT) or eye movement desensitization and reprocessing (EMDR), can help individuals process past experiences and reframe their thought patterns. By addressing the root causes of paranoia, these approaches offer a pathway to recovery, enabling individuals to rebuild trust and reestablish healthier relationships.

Trauma and stress are powerful forces, capable of reshaping the way individuals perceive themselves and the world around them. While their effects can be profound and lasting, with the right tools and support, it is possible to disrupt the cycle of paranoia and foster a more balanced, trusting outlook on life.

How Family Dynamics Affect the Development of Paranoia

The family is often considered the cornerstone of emotional and social development. It is within this environment that individuals first learn about trust, boundaries, and relationships. However, when family dynamics are dysfunctional, they can contribute significantly to the development of paranoia. Certain patterns of interaction within families may foster an atmosphere of mistrust, rigidity, or fear, shaping a child's worldview in ways that predispose them to paranoid tendencies.

Authoritarian Parenting and the Erosion of Autonomy

Children raised under authoritarian or excessively controlling parents often experience a stifling lack of independence. In such households, parents impose strict rules, expect unquestioning obedience, and punish mistakes harshly. These environments instill fear and self-doubt, as children are conditioned to avoid upsetting authority figures at all costs.

Over time, these children may internalize a sense of vulnerability, feeling as though their actions are constantly scrutinized and judged. This hyper-awareness of others' opinions and motives often persists into adulthood, manifesting as chronic suspicion and defensiveness. For example, an adult raised in such a household might interpret constructive criticism at work as a deliberate attack on their competence.

Learned Paranoia Through Observation

Paranoid tendencies can also be modeled and learned within the family setting. When a parent exhibits excessive mistrust, fear of betrayal, or suspicion of others, their behavior serves as a blueprint for how a child perceives and interacts with the world. For instance, if a parent repeatedly warns their child about being deceived or cheated, the child may adopt a worldview where trust is equated with naivety.

This process of observational learning can be particularly impactful if paranoia is a prominent feature of a parent's personality or mental health struggles. A child may grow up believing that suspicion is not only justified but necessary for self-preservation. Over time, this outlook may solidify into a paranoid personality style, making it difficult for the individual to form healthy, trusting relationships.

The Impact of Familial Betrayal

Few experiences shape a child's perception of trust as profoundly as betrayal by a family member. Events such as a parent breaking promises, infidelity between caregivers, or siblings divulging private information can leave lasting psychological scars. These betrayals often send the message that even those who are supposed to protect and support you can hurt you.

This erosion of trust within the family unit may lead to a generalized sense of suspicion. For example, an individual who grew up witnessing a parent's infidelity might struggle to trust romantic partners in adulthood, constantly fearing deception even in stable relationships. These internalized fears, if unchecked, can evolve into pervasive paranoid thought patterns, causing emotional distress and social isolation.

Chronic Conflict and Instability

Families marked by frequent conflict or instability—whether due to financial difficulties, substance abuse, or unresolved interpersonal issues—create an environment of unpredictability. In such settings, children may develop a heightened sensitivity to potential threats, constantly bracing themselves for conflict or harm. This hypervigilance, although adaptive in a chaotic environment, can become maladaptive in adulthood when applied to safer, more predictable situations.

For example, an adult who grew up in a home rife with arguments and secrecy may be quick to assume ulterior motives in others, interpreting neutral actions as deliberate provocations. This constant search for hidden agendas reflects a paranoia rooted in early exposure to familial instability.

Emotional Neglect and Mistrust

Emotional neglect within the family can also contribute to the development of paranoia. When caregivers fail to provide consistent affection, validation, or support, children may feel unworthy of love and attention. This lack of nurturing often leads to feelings of abandonment and a belief that others cannot be relied upon for emotional fulfillment.

As adults, individuals who experienced emotional neglect may approach relationships with skepticism, anticipating rejection or betrayal even when none is present. This defensive posture, while initially protective, can alienate others and perpetuate the cycle of mistrust.

Breaking the Cycle

Understanding the role of family dynamics in shaping paranoia highlights the importance of early intervention and supportive environments. Therapeutic approaches, such as family counseling and individual psychotherapy, can help address underlying wounds and rebuild trust. By fostering healthier communication patterns and challenging maladaptive beliefs, individuals can learn to view relationships through a lens of possibility rather than suspicion.

While the family is often the foundation of trust, it can also be the origin of mistrust. Recognizing the impact of familial experiences on paranoid tendencies is a vital step in breaking free from these patterns and cultivating healthier, more fulfilling relationships.

Cultural Factors in the Expression of Paranoia

Cultural background profoundly shapes how paranoia is experienced, interpreted, and expressed. What may be labeled as paranoia in one cultural context might be viewed as a reasonable response or even a culturally embedded norm in another. This complex interplay between culture and paranoia underscores the need for a nuanced approach to understanding and addressing Paranoid Personality Disorder (PPD).

Collectivist vs. Individualist Societies

The structure and values of a society significantly influence how paranoia manifests. In collectivist cultures, which emphasize group cohesion, interdependence, and communal well-being, paranoia often revolves around fears of damaging relationships or bringing shame to one's family or community. Individuals may become hyperaware of social dynamics, fearing exclusion or judgment from the collective. For example, someone might perceive a casual disagreement as a deliberate attempt to undermine their standing within the group.

In contrast, individualist cultures, which prioritize personal autonomy, independence, and self-expression, tend to frame paranoia around threats to personal freedom and rights. In these contexts, individuals may focus on perceived attempts to control or harm them personally, such as concerns about invasion of privacy or manipulation by others.

Historical and Political Influences

The historical and political experiences of a community play a pivotal role in shaping collective and individual mistrust. In societies that have endured systemic oppression, colonization, or government surveillance, a heightened sense of caution can develop as a survival mechanism. For example, populations that have been subjected to state-sponsored discrimination or targeted violence may cultivate a shared mistrust of authority, which can influence individual behavior and thought patterns.

In such environments, what might be clinically identified as paranoia could instead reflect an adaptive response to genuine threats. A person who grew up in a politically unstable country may be excessively vigilant in protecting themselves or questioning others' motives, behaviors that align with their lived experiences. Recognizing this context is essential for distinguishing between pathological paranoia and realistic caution born out of necessity.

Cultural Stigma Around Mental Health

Attitudes toward mental health vary widely across cultures and play a critical role in the recognition and management of paranoia. In cultures where mental health issues are stigmatized, individuals with PPD may feel pressure to conceal their struggles, fearing judgment or ostracism. This suppression of symptoms can intensify feelings of isolation and mistrust, reinforcing the patterns associated with paranoia.

Additionally, some cultures may attribute paranoid thoughts or behaviors to spiritual or supernatural causes, such as curses or possession, rather than recognizing them as symptoms of a mental health condition. These interpretations can delay or prevent individuals from seeking professional help, leaving the disorder unaddressed and potentially worsening over time.

Cultural Sensitivity in Treatment

Effective care for individuals with PPD requires an understanding of cultural influences on their perceptions and behaviors. For instance, clinicians working with individuals from collectivist societies should consider the role of family and community dynamics in shaping their fears, while those treating individuals from historically oppressed communities should be mindful of the impact of systemic injustices on their worldview.

Culturally sensitive approaches not only help avoid misdiagnoses but also foster trust between the individual and the clinician—a critical factor when working with individuals prone to suspicion. Integrating cultural awareness into treatment ensures that care is both effective and respectful, allowing individuals to feel seen and understood within their unique contexts.

Bridging Cultural and Clinical Perspectives

Understanding the cultural dimensions of paranoia highlights the importance of viewing PPD through a multifaceted lens. Paranoia is not simply a fixed set of symptoms but a dynamic interplay of personality, experience, and cultural context. By acknowledging these influences, mental health professionals can better differentiate between adaptive behaviors rooted in cultural realities and pathological paranoia, paving the way for more compassionate and effective interventions.

The Influence of Substance Abuse on Paranoia

Substance abuse can play a significant role in both the development and exacerbation of paranoia. The connection between substance use and paranoid thought patterns is multifaceted, involving neurochemical disruptions, the psychological effects of addiction, and the challenges associated with substance-dependent lifestyles. This interplay can intensify the symptoms of Paranoid Personality Disorder (PPD) or even induce paranoia in those without a prior history of the condition.

Neurochemical Disruptions

Many substances alter brain chemistry in ways that can lead to heightened suspicion or delusional thinking. Stimulants such as cocaine and methamphetamine are notorious for their impact on the brain's dopamine system. These drugs increase dopamine levels, which, in moderate amounts, enhance motivation and reward but, in excess, can cause paranoid delusions or hallucinations. Long-term or heavy use often results in a persistent state of hypervigilance, even when the drug is no longer in the system.

Similarly, hallucinogens such as LSD or psilocybin can distort perception and induce paranoia during the experience, especially in individuals predisposed to anxiety or mistrust. Even substances like alcohol, typically considered a depressant, can have paradoxical effects. Chronic alcohol use or withdrawal often exacerbates feelings of anxiety and mistrust, particularly in individuals using it to self-medicate for preexisting paranoia.

Cannabis and Paranoia

Cannabis is one of the most commonly cited substances linked to paranoia. High doses, particularly of strains rich in THC, can disrupt normal thought patterns, leading to temporary episodes of paranoia or heightened suspicion. For individuals predisposed to PPD or anxiety disorders, cannabis use can act as a trigger, intensifying their symptoms and impairing their ability to distinguish between real and perceived threats.

Lifestyle Instability

Beyond neurochemical effects, substance abuse introduces significant lifestyle instability, which can reinforce paranoid tendencies. Individuals struggling with addiction often face financial difficulties, legal troubles, and strained relationships, creating a chaotic and unpredictable environment. This instability can heighten feelings of mistrust and alienation, leading to a vicious cycle where paranoia and substance abuse feed into one another.

For example, someone living with addiction may develop genuine concerns about being judged, betrayed, or harmed by others, which are then magnified by their altered brain chemistry. These fears may appear rational in the context of their environment but can spiral into full-blown paranoid delusions over time.

Co-Occurring Mental Health Conditions

Substance abuse frequently coexists with other mental health conditions, such as depression, anxiety, or trauma-related disorders. These underlying issues often serve as the initial motivation for substance use but can also intensify feelings of mistrust and suspicion. For individuals with PPD, the addition of substance abuse can complicate treatment and recovery, as the interplay between paranoia and addiction creates a multifaceted challenge.

Breaking the Cycle

Substance-induced paranoia underscores the importance of addressing both addiction and underlying mental health conditions in tandem. Interventions that focus solely on one aspect often fall short, as the two issues are deeply intertwined. Comprehensive treatment approaches that combine detoxification, psychotherapy, and social support can help individuals break the cycle of addiction while simultaneously addressing their paranoid thought patterns.

By examining the influence of substance abuse on paranoia, a more complete picture of PPD emerges. The complex relationship between neurochemistry, lifestyle, and mental health highlights both the challenges and opportunities for intervention. As we move forward in exploring potential solutions, it becomes clear that understanding these contributing factors is key to offering effective support and paving the way for recovery.

Chapter 4: Diagnosing Paranoid Personality Disorder

Diagnosing Paranoid Personality Disorder (PPD) is a delicate process that demands attention to detail and a thorough understanding of the disorder's intricacies. PPD is characterized by deep-seated mistrust and suspicion of others, often without a justifiable basis. These patterns of thinking and behavior are persistent and affect nearly all aspects of an individual's life, making it a condition that requires careful evaluation.

The diagnostic process is not straightforward, as PPD shares overlapping symptoms with several other mental health disorders, such as schizophrenia, schizotypal personality disorder, and anxiety disorders. This overlap necessitates a detailed differential diagnosis to distinguish PPD from conditions with similar features. For instance, while paranoia is common across these disorders, the nature and context of the symptoms vary significantly. In PPD, paranoia is a chronic personality trait, whereas in schizophrenia, it is often episodic and accompanied by delusions or hallucinations.

A cornerstone of diagnosis lies in adhering to the criteria established by the Diagnostic and Statistical Manual of Mental Disorders, Fifth Edition (DSM-5). According to the DSM-5, PPD involves a pervasive pattern of distrust and suspicion beginning in early adulthood, evidenced by specific behavioral and cognitive tendencies. These include reluctance to confide in others, misinterpreting benign remarks as threatening, holding persistent grudges, and harboring unjustified doubts about the loyalty of friends or partners. For a diagnosis to be made, these traits must significantly impair functioning and not result from other medical conditions, substance use, or psychotic disorders.

Emerging approaches are enriching the diagnostic landscape for PPD, incorporating advancements in technology and interdisciplinary insights. Neuroimaging studies, for instance, are being explored to understand the neural mechanisms underlying hypervigilance and mistrust. Psychometric tools are also being refined to provide a more objective and comprehensive assessment of paranoid traits. Meanwhile, artificial intelligence and machine learning are being piloted to analyze speech patterns, social interactions, and behavioral data, which may reveal subtle indicators of PPD.

Mental health professionals play an essential role in the diagnostic journey. Establishing trust is particularly challenging in PPD cases, as individuals often view clinicians with suspicion. The assessment process involves a combination of clinical interviews, behavioral observations, and validated diagnostic tools. When possible, collateral information from family members or close associates can offer valuable context, although it must be managed delicately to avoid exacerbating the individual's distrust.

Despite advancements, diagnosing PPD remains challenging. Individuals with the disorder are often reluctant to seek help, as their mistrust extends to healthcare providers. Early symptoms may also be mistaken for personality traits, such as caution or independence, delaying intervention. Co-occurring disorders, such as depression or anxiety, can further complicate the diagnostic picture. Stigma surrounding mental health often compounds these issues, discouraging individuals from acknowledging their struggles.

Accurate and timely diagnosis is critical to providing appropriate care and support for individuals with PPD. By employing a careful, empathetic, and evidence-based approach, clinicians can navigate the complexities of PPD, paving the way for effective treatment and improved quality of life. As our understanding of the disorder continues to evolve, so too will the tools and strategies available to aid in its diagnosis.

The Diagnostic Criteria in DSM-5

The Diagnostic and Statistical Manual of Mental Disorders (DSM-5) serves as a crucial guide for the identification and classification of mental health conditions, including Paranoid Personality Disorder (PPD). The criteria outlined in the DSM-5 help clinicians differentiate PPD from other disorders, providing a standardized approach to diagnosis.

PPD is primarily defined by a pervasive pattern of distrust and suspicion toward others, with individuals interpreting their motives as malicious or harmful, even in the absence of evidence. This suspicion often extends to all areas of life, affecting personal relationships, work environments, and social interactions. For an individual to be diagnosed with PPD, they must exhibit at least four of the following criteria:

1. **Unfounded suspicion of others** – Individuals with PPD are often preoccupied with the belief that others are attempting to exploit, deceive, or harm them, despite lacking solid proof to support these fears.
2. **Doubts about the loyalty or trustworthiness of friends and associates** – A pervasive sense of mistrust leads them to question the motives of those around them, even in close personal

relationships, often without any substantial reason.

3. **Reluctance to confide in others** – Because of the fear that information shared will be used against them, people with PPD may avoid opening up, even to those they are closest to. This fear of betrayal prevents the development of healthy communication and emotional intimacy.

4. **Reading hidden threats or meanings into benign remarks or events** – An individual with PPD may misinterpret ordinary interactions, attributing negative, often harmful, intent to others' words or actions, even when no such threat is present.

5. **Persistent grudges** – People with PPD tend to hold onto past slights, whether real or imagined, for extended periods. They may find it difficult to forgive perceived wrongs, reinforcing their suspicion and resentment.

6. **Perceptions of unwarranted attacks** – They may believe that others are attacking their character or reputation, even when there is no evidence to support this belief. This often leads to a heightened emotional response, such as anger or retaliation, and further alienates them from others.

7. **Unjustified suspicion of a partner's fidelity** – An individual with PPD might constantly doubt

their partner's loyalty or commitment, often without any legitimate cause, leading to strain in romantic relationships.

For a diagnosis of PPD to be made, these symptoms must be chronic, persisting for at least six months or longer, and must significantly impair the individual's ability to function in daily life. This includes challenges in forming and maintaining relationships, difficulties in the workplace, and problems engaging socially. It is essential that these symptoms cannot be attributed to other mental health conditions, such as delusional disorder or schizophrenia, nor should they be the result of substance abuse or medical conditions.

In the context of the DSM-5, it's critical to distinguish between generalized suspiciousness—a trait shared by many individuals—and paranoia, which is persistent, disproportionate, and all-encompassing. The DSM-5 emphasizes that for a true diagnosis of PPD, the degree of impairment caused by these beliefs must be significant enough to hinder normal functioning. This comprehensive criteria framework helps mental health professionals assess and diagnose PPD with accuracy, ensuring that the individual receives appropriate treatment.

Differential Diagnosis: PPD vs. Schizophrenia and Other Disorders

Accurate diagnosis of Paranoid Personality Disorder (PPD) is essential, as its symptoms can overlap with several other mental health conditions. Distinguishing PPD from similar disorders ensures the correct treatment approach is taken. While paranoia is a central feature of PPD, it is not the only disorder where suspicious thoughts emerge. Below, we explore how PPD compares with other conditions, such as schizophrenia, schizotypal personality disorder, borderline personality disorder, and anxiety disorders, to better understand their key differences.

PPD vs. Schizophrenia

Although both PPD and schizophrenia can involve paranoia, there are significant distinctions between the two. Schizophrenia is primarily characterized by a break with reality, manifesting through hallucinations (e.g., hearing voices or seeing things that aren't there) and delusions (strongly held false beliefs, such as believing one is being persecuted or controlled). These symptoms are not present in PPD.

Additionally, paranoia in schizophrenia tends to be episodic, often occurring during active psychotic episodes, whereas in PPD, paranoia is a chronic and enduring pattern of thought that permeates the individual's life. Individuals with PPD maintain a firm belief in their suspicions even when faced with contradictory evidence, making it a more persistent and stable trait compared to the fleeting and episodic nature of paranoia in schizophrenia.

PPD vs. Schizotypal Personality Disorder

At first glance, schizotypal personality disorder (STPD) may seem similar to PPD due to the presence of paranoia. However, there are key differences between the two. While individuals with STPD do experience suspiciousness, they are also often marked by eccentric behavior, odd beliefs, and magical thinking—such as believing in the supernatural or having unusual perceptual experiences. These features distinguish STPD from PPD, where eccentricity and magical thinking are not central traits.

In STPD, the paranoid thoughts are usually accompanied by social detachment, odd speech patterns, and other characteristics that reflect a deep social and cognitive disconnect, which is not typical in PPD. People with PPD are primarily focused on issues of trust and distrust of others, without the broader range of oddities seen in schizotypal individuals.

PPD vs. Borderline Personality Disorder

Both PPD and borderline personality disorder (BPD) involve significant challenges in interpersonal relationships, but the nature of the difficulties is different. In BPD, individuals struggle with emotional instability, intense fears of abandonment, and impulsive behaviors—all of which are less central to PPD.

Paranoia in BPD often occurs in response to perceived threats to relationships, such as fearing abandonment by a partner or friend, and it tends to fluctuate with the individual's emotional state. On the other hand, in PPD, the paranoia is more generalized and is not dependent on specific relational triggers. It stems from a broader, deeply ingrained belief that others are untrustworthy or have malicious intent, regardless of their actions.

Furthermore, BPD is marked by significant mood swings, self-image issues, and impulsivity, none of which are characteristic of PPD. In PPD, the primary issue is enduring suspicion and distrust, not emotional dysregulation or impulsivity.

PPD vs. Anxiety Disorders

Anxiety disorders can also involve feelings of fear and mistrust, but the paranoia in these disorders typically arises from fear of harm or insecurity rather than an intrinsic belief that others are intentionally harmful. For instance, in generalized anxiety disorder or social anxiety disorder, individuals might worry about being judged or criticized, but their concerns are usually focused on specific situations or scenarios.

In contrast, the paranoia seen in PPD is deeply rooted in a generalized mistrust of others. It goes beyond situational anxiety and reflects a consistent worldview where the individual sees others as inherently untrustworthy or potentially harmful. While someone with anxiety might fear a potential threat in certain contexts, a person with PPD may see threats everywhere, often in innocuous or neutral situations.

The process of differentiating PPD from other mental health conditions, such as schizophrenia, schizotypal personality disorder, borderline personality disorder, and anxiety disorders, requires careful attention to both the symptoms and the context in which they occur. By clearly identifying these distinctions, mental health professionals can make more accurate diagnoses, ensuring that individuals receive the most appropriate care and treatment tailored to their specific needs.

Emerging Approaches to Diagnosing PPD

In recent years, advancements in psychology and neuroscience have paved the way for new and innovative approaches to diagnosing Paranoid Personality Disorder (PPD). Traditional diagnostic methods primarily rely on clinical observation and self-reported symptoms, but emerging methodologies aim to enhance diagnostic accuracy, offer deeper insights into the disorder's underlying mechanisms, and minimize subjectivity in assessment. These approaches integrate technological innovations and interdisciplinary frameworks, promising more nuanced and reliable diagnoses of PPD.

Neuroimaging Studies

One of the most exciting developments in the field of PPD diagnosis is the use of neuroimaging techniques, such as functional magnetic resonance imaging (fMRI). These methods allow researchers to observe brain activity in real-time, particularly in regions associated with emotions, cognition, and social interactions. In the context of PPD, fMRI studies are exploring whether patterns of brain activation differ in individuals with paranoid tendencies, especially in areas linked to suspicion, hypervigilance, and threat detection.

For example, neuroimaging could potentially reveal heightened activity in the amygdala, the brain's center for processing fear and emotional responses, suggesting an overactive response to perceived threats. Though these studies are still in the early stages, they hold promise for uncovering the neurological underpinnings of paranoia, providing objective data that could complement traditional diagnostic methods and lead to more precise treatment interventions.

Psychometric Tools

To reduce the subjectivity inherent in diagnosing PPD through interviews and self-report questionnaires, new psychometric tools are being developed. These tools aim to measure paranoia, mistrust, and suspicion with greater accuracy. Self-report questionnaires and behavioral assessments are being refined to assess the individual's level of trust in others and their tendency to perceive benign actions as threatening.

For example, the Paranoia Checklist and other structured diagnostic tools offer a more systematic way to evaluate the severity and consistency of paranoid thoughts. These tools are designed to provide a more comprehensive picture of the individual's experiences, helping clinicians distinguish between transient fears and pervasive, pathological paranoia. The goal is to create reliable, standardized assessments that can be used in both clinical and research settings, ensuring that the diagnosis of PPD is based on a more objective and holistic understanding of the person's symptoms.

Machine Learning and AI

The field of artificial intelligence (AI) and machine learning is also making strides in diagnosing PPD. By analyzing large datasets of speech patterns, behavioral cues, and social interactions, AI systems are being trained to detect subtle signs of paranoia that may not be easily recognized by human clinicians. These technologies can analyze linguistic patterns, tone of voice, and non-verbal communication to identify indicators of distrust or suspicious thinking.

For instance, machine learning algorithms could be trained to flag changes in an individual's speech, such as increased defensiveness, social withdrawal, or verbal signs of suspicion. Additionally, AI tools could be applied to analyze social media activity, online interactions, or interviews, helping clinicians identify potential signs of PPD in real-world settings. While these technologies show great potential, they are still in the developmental phase and require further validation before they can be reliably used in clinical practice.

As the field of psychology continues to evolve, so too does our understanding of Paranoid Personality Disorder.

The integration of neuroimaging, psychometric tools, and machine learning into the diagnostic process offers exciting new possibilities for identifying PPD with greater precision. These emerging approaches hold the potential to improve not only diagnosis but also treatment, by providing more objective data and insights into the underlying mechanisms of paranoia. However, much research is still needed to validate these methods, ensuring that they are reliable, ethical, and effective in clinical practice. Ultimately, these innovations point to a future where diagnosing PPD is more accurate, personalized, and informed by a comprehensive understanding of the individual's psychological and neurological makeup.

The Role of Mental Health Professionals in Assessment

Mental health professionals are essential in the assessment and diagnosis of Paranoid Personality Disorder (PPD), yet their role is made particularly challenging by the nature of the disorder itself. PPD is rooted in a pervasive distrust and suspicion of others, which often extends to clinicians. This inherent mistrust makes it difficult for individuals with PPD to form a therapeutic alliance with healthcare providers, a critical component of the assessment process. Establishing rapport is a delicate balance for mental health professionals, as they must remain neutral, non-judgmental, and empathetic while navigating the individual's reluctance to engage openly.

A key component of the diagnostic process is the thorough use of clinical interviews, which allow clinicians to gather detailed information about the individual's history, thought patterns, and behaviors. These interviews typically focus on understanding the person's worldview, how they perceive relationships, and their responses to perceived threats or betrayals. Given the distrust inherent in PPD, individuals may be less forthcoming in these interviews, providing only partial information or interpreting questions in a suspicious light. In these cases, open-ended questions and a non-confrontational style of communication can encourage the person to share more willingly, even if cautiously.

Behavioral observations are another valuable tool in assessing PPD. These observations occur during the interview and in more natural settings, helping clinicians evaluate how the person interacts with others and how they react to various situations. Are they overly guarded? Do they exhibit signs of defensiveness or withdrawal? These behaviors often point to patterns of thought and distrust that characterize the disorder. Over time, these observations can provide crucial evidence to complement the information gathered through interviews.

In addition to interviews and observations, validated assessment tools are often used to provide a more objective measure of paranoid traits. These tools, such as self-report questionnaires and personality inventories, are designed to quantify the presence and severity of paranoid thinking. Though these assessments are helpful, it's important to remember that individuals with PPD may respond defensively to these tools, answering questions in ways that further reinforce their suspicions. Therefore, careful interpretation of these results, within the broader context of clinical judgment, is essential.

Collaboration with family members or close associates can provide additional insights, but this step must be handled with great sensitivity. People with PPD often feel betrayed or threatened when others speak about them, especially in a therapeutic context. Mental health professionals must ensure that any involvement of family members is done in a way that respects the individual's privacy and minimizes the risk of exacerbating their feelings of mistrust. It is crucial that clinicians gain the patient's consent before contacting family members or close associates and that these individuals are engaged with the understanding that the goal is to support the individual in their healing process.

Despite the challenges, mental health professionals are in a unique position to diagnose and support individuals with PPD. By combining empathetic communication, careful observation, evidence-based assessments, and collaboration with trusted individuals, clinicians can overcome many of the barriers to effective diagnosis. These professionals also have the training and expertise to recognize the complexities of PPD, differentiating it from other conditions with overlapping symptoms. Their role in identifying the disorder is not just about gathering information but also about building trust over time—enabling them to provide the most effective interventions and support for individuals living with PPD.

Challenges in Early Detection and Diagnosis

Diagnosing Paranoid Personality Disorder (PPD) in its early stages presents unique and significant challenges, primarily due to the inherent nature of the disorder itself and the context in which it manifests. Several factors complicate the diagnostic process and contribute to delayed intervention.

Mistrust of Clinicians

One of the most significant hurdles in diagnosing PPD early is the mistrust individuals with the disorder often feel toward mental health professionals. Given that paranoia is defined by suspicion and distrust of others' motives, people with PPD may be unwilling to seek professional help in the first place. They may view clinicians as part of a larger system of perceived threats or feel that the very process of diagnosis is an attempt to control or manipulate them. This reluctance to engage with professionals leads to delays in identifying the disorder, often until symptoms are severe or a crisis point has been reached. As a result, individuals may suffer for longer periods without appropriate intervention or support.

Overlap with Normal Personality Traits

Another challenge in diagnosing PPD early is the overlap between paranoid tendencies and normal personality traits. For example, caution, independence, and skepticism are healthy personality traits in certain situations, particularly when it comes to protecting oneself or questioning unverified information. These traits, when taken to an extreme, can appear similar to the early warning signs of PPD. A person who is generally cautious or prefers to work alone may not seem significantly different from someone with a more pervasive mistrust of others. The line between adaptive skepticism and pathological suspicion is often blurred in the early stages, making it difficult to discern whether these traits are simply part of the individual's personality or indicative of a deeper, more pervasive disorder.

Stigma and Societal Barriers

The stigma surrounding mental health also plays a crucial role in delaying diagnosis. In many cultures, there is still a significant social stigma attached to seeking help for psychological disorders. This stigma can deter individuals from acknowledging their symptoms, fearing judgment or discrimination. In the case of PPD, where individuals are already suspicious of others' motives, the societal pressure to avoid seeking help may exacerbate their feelings of alienation. The reluctance to admit there is a problem or seek help, compounded by fear of being labeled as mentally ill, can result in significant delays in diagnosis and treatment.

Co-occurring Disorders

Many individuals with PPD experience co-occurring mental health conditions, such as anxiety, depression, or substance use disorders. These overlapping conditions can obscure the symptoms of paranoia, leading to misdiagnosis or a focus on treating the more immediately apparent issues. For instance, a person with both PPD and depression may be more likely to seek help for feelings of sadness and hopelessness rather than the underlying paranoia. Similarly, anxiety disorders and substance use can exacerbate the symptoms of PPD, further complicating the diagnostic picture. The presence of co-occurring disorders requires clinicians to carefully differentiate between symptoms that arise from multiple sources, which can be challenging in the absence of a comprehensive diagnostic approach.

Addressing the Challenges

To overcome these challenges, there is a need for increased awareness of PPD among both the general public and healthcare professionals. Early identification of the disorder relies on professionals being attuned to its subtle signs and differences from other conditions. Additionally, better screening tools are crucial. These tools must be designed to accurately detect PPD without reinforcing the individual's mistrust or exacerbating their defensive behaviors.

Building trust is equally vital. Mental health professionals working with individuals who have PPD must be patient, empathetic, and non-confrontational. Taking a slow, methodical approach that respects the individual's sense of autonomy can help to establish a working relationship, even in the face of suspicion. Psychoeducation and interventions that emphasize the benefits of seeking help, while validating the person's experiences, can also encourage individuals to engage in the diagnostic process and begin their path to treatment.

The diagnostic process for Paranoid Personality Disorder is complex and requires both clinical expertise and a deep understanding of the unique challenges posed by the disorder. Professionals must carefully distinguish between normal skepticism and pathological paranoia while taking into account the overlapping symptoms of co-occurring disorders. Despite the difficulties, early detection and accurate diagnosis are essential for ensuring timely and effective intervention. With the right tools, awareness, and approaches, mental health professionals can provide the necessary support for individuals with PPD, helping them navigate the challenges of the disorder and improve their quality of life.

Chapter 5: Understanding the Paranoid Mind

Understanding the paranoid mind requires a deep exploration of the internal landscape of those living with Paranoid Personality Disorder (PPD). This disorder significantly shapes how individuals perceive, interpret, and respond to the world around them. Often, it is a world seen through a lens of suspicion, fear, and defensiveness. The cognitive processes, emotional reactions, and distorted perceptions that define PPD create a unique experience, one that is marked by constant vigilance, mistrust, and a sense of threat that others may not perceive.

At the core of this experience are cognitive distortions—deeply ingrained, inaccurate ways of thinking that influence how individuals with PPD make sense of their interactions. These distortions, like seeing benign actions as hostile or interpreting neutral comments as personal attacks, skew their worldview, reinforcing the belief that the world is a dangerous place where others cannot be trusted. The constant reinterpretation of everyday events through this warped lens often leads to a cycle of increasing paranoia and isolation.

Coupled with these cognitive distortions is hypervigilance, a heightened state of alertness where every action and word is scrutinized for potential threats. This constant state of readiness to defend oneself or react to perceived danger can be exhausting and emotionally draining. For those with PPD, every interaction feels like a potential landmine, where hidden meanings and secret agendas lie just beneath the surface of simple conversations or behaviors.

In more severe cases, delusional thinking may take hold, where the individual becomes convinced of false beliefs—such as the notion that people are conspiring against them or attempting to harm them in ways that have no factual basis. These delusions are not easily swayed by logic or reason, as they are deeply rooted in the individual's sense of vulnerability and fear of betrayal.

Finally, the emotional toll of living with paranoia cannot be understated. The relentless suspicion and mistrust can lead to intense feelings of isolation, anxiety, and emotional exhaustion. Relationships suffer as others may struggle to understand the constant need for reassurance or the inability to trust even the most well-intentioned gestures. The emotional burden of paranoia also manifests in feelings of inadequacy and frustration, as individuals with PPD are often unable to break free from the cycle of fear and doubt that consumes them.

Cognitive Distortions and Perceptions of Threat

At the heart of Paranoid Personality Disorder is a pattern of cognitive distortions—flawed ways of thinking that lead individuals to consistently misinterpret the intentions of others. These distorted thought patterns often revolve around perceiving others as threatening, deceitful, or hostile, even when no clear evidence supports these beliefs.

One common cognitive distortion seen in PPD is mind reading, where an individual believes they can read others' thoughts and intentions, typically assuming the worst. For example, a person with PPD may interpret a casual comment from a colleague as an attack, even though the comment was likely neutral or benign. Catastrophizing, another cognitive distortion, involves expecting the worst possible outcome, such as assuming that a minor misunderstanding will escalate into a full-blown conflict or betrayal. These cognitive patterns reinforce the belief that the world is filled with dangers and that others cannot be trusted.

These distorted perceptions of threat are not merely occasional but are persistent and pervasive, coloring the way individuals with PPD view the world. This constant suspicion can result in a life lived on the defensive, constantly interpreting even neutral interactions through the lens of distrust and fear.

The distortions reinforce each other, creating a cycle that can be difficult to break. For example, when a person with PPD misinterprets others' actions and responds defensively, those around them may begin to act more distant or wary, unintentionally reinforcing the paranoid individual's beliefs. This cycle deepens their sense of isolation and strengthens their conviction that others are, indeed, untrustworthy and harmful.

As a result, these cognitive distortions can severely impact relationships, social interactions, and daily functioning. The person with PPD becomes trapped in a world of perceived threats, unable to see others' true intentions or engage in healthy, trust-based relationships. It's this skewed lens through which they view the world that makes paranoia so persistent and challenging to overcome.

Hypervigilance and Mistrust: The Foundation of Paranoia

Hypervigilance, a heightened state of alertness, is a defining characteristic of Paranoid Personality Disorder (PPD). Individuals with PPD are often in a constant state of watchfulness, always on the lookout for signs of danger, betrayal, or deception in their interactions. This vigilance becomes a deeply ingrained habit, influencing how they navigate the world around them. It requires them to remain constantly alert, scrutinizing others' words and actions for any hint of malice, real or imagined.

At the core of this hypervigilance lies profound mistrust. Those with PPD find it exceedingly difficult to believe that others have good or benign intentions. Even the most innocent gestures or neutral comments are often perceived as covert attempts to deceive, manipulate, or harm. They live in a world where everyone and everything is suspect, making it nearly impossible to foster meaningful or trusting relationships.

This mistrust extends to every aspect of their social life, from personal relationships to professional interactions. People with PPD might read between the lines of a casual conversation, interpreting words and body language as signs of hidden motives. This constant questioning of others' intentions can create an emotional distance that isolates them, preventing them from engaging fully with others. It may lead to defensive reactions, such as avoiding social gatherings or maintaining a rigid stance in conversations, always prepared for what they believe is an inevitable betrayal.

The hypervigilance experienced by individuals with PPD is often disproportionate to the actual level of threat. In many cases, there is no real danger, yet the individual remains on edge, unable to turn off their heightened suspicion. This can manifest in compulsive behaviors, such as checking emails repeatedly for signs of betrayal, overanalyzing casual remarks, or avoiding situations where they feel they may be judged. These actions, while protective in their intent, only reinforce the individual's belief that others are out to harm them, deepening the cycle of mistrust.

The emotional toll of living in a constant state of alertness is profound. Individuals with PPD often experience significant anxiety, stress, and exhaustion, as they struggle to maintain their defenses. There is little room for relaxation or genuine connection, leaving them unable to experience the sense of safety or comfort that is essential for emotional well-being. The persistent hypervigilance can erode their mental health, making it even harder to break free from the pervasive sense of distrust that defines the disorder.

The Role of Delusional Thinking

In more severe cases of Paranoid Personality Disorder (PPD), delusional thinking can emerge, adding a significant layer of complexity to the disorder. Delusions are fixed, false beliefs that are disconnected from reality, and they play a central role in various mental health conditions, such as schizophrenia and delusional disorder. In the context of PPD, these delusions often center around the belief that others are conspiring to harm or deceive the individual.

For example, someone with PPD might become convinced that their coworkers are secretly plotting against them, undermining their reputation or career behind their back. They might believe that family members are deliberately withholding important information or conspiring to mislead them. These beliefs can appear to be irrational to outsiders, but to the individual with PPD, they feel profoundly real and threatening.

The hallmark of these delusions is their resistance to logic or evidence. Even when presented with clear counterarguments or reassurance from others, individuals with PPD often cling to their beliefs, as they are deeply rooted in a pervasive mistrust of the world around them. The delusions serve as a lens through which they interpret all interactions, further reinforcing their suspicions and sense of danger. This makes it incredibly challenging for them to trust others or to accept alternative perspectives.

Delusional thinking can profoundly impact an individual's social life and relationships. As the delusions become more entrenched, the individual may become increasingly withdrawn, defensive, and isolated. They may reject any attempts by friends, family, or colleagues to offer comfort or clarification, as they view these gestures with suspicion, believing them to be part of the conspiracy. This creates a barrier that prevents meaningful communication and deepens the cycle of paranoia.

The distress caused by delusional thinking is significant. The inability to distinguish between real threats and imagined ones can create constant emotional turmoil. The individual may experience heightened anxiety, fear, and confusion, unable to trust their own perceptions. In some cases, these delusions can lead to behaviors that are disproportionate to the perceived threat. For instance, they may confront others aggressively, make accusations without evidence, or engage in actions that alienate those around them. These behaviors, while often driven by the need to protect themselves from imagined harm, can have damaging consequences for their relationships and social functioning.

Ultimately, the presence of delusional thinking in PPD exacerbates the disorder, further isolating the individual and making it more difficult to break free from the grip of paranoia. Without intervention, these delusions can take on a life of their own, driving the person deeper into a world of mistrust and fear, and reinforcing their belief that they are surrounded by enemies.

How the World Appears to Someone with PPD

For someone living with Paranoid Personality Disorder (PPD), the world often appears as a threatening, unpredictable place. Every day, interactions that most people would view as neutral or positive are instead interpreted through a lens of suspicion. Individuals with PPD tend to perceive social exchanges as covert attempts at manipulation, deception, or betrayal. Every conversation is carefully examined for hidden meanings, and even the smallest gesture can be scrutinized for signs of malicious intent.

This distorted view of reality significantly impacts how someone with PPD experiences the world. A harmless comment from a friend might be seen as an insult, and a friendly smile could be misinterpreted as a sign of contempt or mockery. These misreadings of everyday interactions are often rooted in an overwhelming need for self-protection, as individuals with PPD anticipate harm from others before it even occurs. This heightened vigilance leads them to constantly question the motives of those around them, further intensifying their paranoia.

Trust becomes an incredibly difficult concept for someone with PPD to grasp. They may find it hard to trust anyone, including close friends or family members. The fear that others may be deceiving or plotting against them overshadows any attempts to build meaningful relationships. As a result, their connections with others are often fraught with tension, misunderstandings, and conflict. In intimate relationships, this lack of trust can create a sense of distance and alienation, making it hard to experience emotional intimacy or vulnerability.

For those with PPD, the world is not a place filled with potential allies or support. It is more like a battleground where every interaction carries the potential for conflict or harm. This constant state of hyperawareness and suspicion can be mentally and emotionally exhausting, draining the individual's energy and leaving little room for positive experiences or peaceful moments. The emotional toll of this outlook can lead to a pervasive sense of isolation, as the person feels unable to connect with others in a genuine or trusting way.

Living with PPD means being in a perpetual state of emotional turmoil, where the fear of betrayal and the need for self-defense dominate the individual's worldview. This relentless vigilance and mistrust color every aspect of their life, making it difficult to experience the world as a safe and supportive environment. Instead, they are left feeling alone, misunderstood, and often overwhelmed by their own heightened sense of danger.

The Emotional Toll of Living with Paranoia

Living with paranoia is an emotionally draining experience. The constant vigilance required to monitor every interaction, anticipate threats, and protect oneself from perceived harm generates high levels of anxiety and stress. Individuals with Paranoid Personality Disorder (PPD) are often in a heightened state of alertness, which leaves them physically and mentally exhausted. The need to stay on guard at all times prevents them from experiencing moments of calm or peace, making their emotional world feel unrelenting and exhausting.

The inability to trust others or feel secure in relationships deepens the emotional burden of PPD. It is not uncommon for individuals with this disorder to feel isolated, disconnected, and lonely. Their mistrust leads them to withdraw from others, often pushing loved ones, friends, and even colleagues away, leaving them without the support systems most people rely on for comfort and reassurance. As a result, feelings of depression can easily take root, intensifying the emotional strain.

Anger and frustration are also common emotional responses for individuals with PPD. The constant suspicion and defensiveness can make it seem as though others are constantly betraying or judging them. This can lead to repeated feelings of being misunderstood, which only heightens their belief that the world is against them. Even minor, innocuous comments or actions from others can be perceived as slights or attacks, further intensifying feelings of resentment and alienation.

The emotional impact of PPD also manifests in self-esteem issues. Because individuals with this disorder often feel scrutinized and judged, they may develop a sense of inadequacy or inferiority. These feelings are compounded by their inability to trust that others have good intentions, leading them to second-guess their own worth and question their value in relationships or social interactions. This internal struggle can leave them feeling trapped in a cycle of self-doubt and defensiveness, making it difficult to achieve a sense of peace or self-acceptance.

Relationships, whether personal or professional, often bear the brunt of the emotional toll of paranoia. The constant tension and suspicion inherent in PPD can lead to frequent conflicts with others. Friends, family, and colleagues may feel confused or frustrated by the individual's behavior, which often results in misunderstandings and estrangement. As individuals with PPD push others away out of fear of betrayal, they inadvertently deepen their isolation and feelings of loneliness. This, in turn, reinforces the negative cycle of mistrust and alienation, which continues to take a toll on their emotional well-being.

Ultimately, living with paranoia is not just about cognitive patterns of suspicion; it is an emotional struggle that affects nearly every facet of life. The pervasive sense of fear, mistrust, and isolation can feel suffocating, leaving individuals feeling trapped in their own minds. Their emotional experiences are often colored by the belief that others are out to deceive or harm them, creating a world that is not only unsafe but emotionally taxing. It is crucial to understand the emotional complexities of PPD to provide the support and care necessary to help individuals navigate these challenges, rebuild trust, and regain a sense of balance in their lives.

The internal experience of Paranoid Personality Disorder is a complex web of cognitive distortions, emotional pain, and mistrust. For those living with PPD, the world is perceived as hostile and untrustworthy, with every interaction viewed through a lens of suspicion. The emotional toll of this disorder extends far beyond the cognitive distortions, influencing self-esteem, relationships, and overall mental health. By understanding these emotional dynamics, it becomes possible to offer more effective support, helping individuals with PPD navigate the turmoil of their inner world and begin to heal.

Chapter 6: Relationships and Paranoid Personality Disorder

Relationships are a cornerstone of human experience, providing the foundation for emotional connection, shared growth, and mutual support. For most, these bonds offer a sense of security and belonging. However, for individuals living with Paranoid Personality Disorder (PPD), relationships often take on an entirely different and more challenging dynamic. The pervasive distrust and defensiveness that define PPD can transform what should be a source of comfort into a persistent battleground of suspicion and tension.

For those with PPD, relationships are fraught with complexity. The disorder's hallmark characteristics—chronic mistrust, a tendency to misinterpret others' actions, and a fear of betrayal—create obstacles that can erode even the strongest connections. While relationships with romantic partners, family members, and friends may begin with the same potential for closeness as anyone else's, the ever-present lens of suspicion often leads to conflict, distance, and emotional strain.

In romantic partnerships, the challenges of PPD manifest through jealousy, fear of infidelity, and constant doubt about the partner's intentions. This creates a cycle where efforts to reassure and maintain peace are overshadowed by relentless questioning and perceived slights. Similarly, familial and platonic relationships are often tested by the individual's inclination to view even innocent actions or comments as veiled criticisms or betrayals. Friends and family members may find themselves walking on eggshells, unsure of how to navigate these dynamics without exacerbating the tension.

Beyond personal relationships, PPD significantly impacts professional and social interactions. In the workplace, mistrust of colleagues and supervisors can hinder collaboration and productivity, while social gatherings may feel overwhelming or unsafe, leading to withdrawal or avoidance. The inability to trust others or feel secure in relationships often leaves individuals with PPD isolated, which further entrenches their feelings of alienation and defensiveness.

Understanding the unique challenges that individuals with PPD face in relationships is crucial for offering meaningful support. By examining the nuances of how paranoia influences romantic, familial, and professional dynamics, this chapter sheds light on the ways PPD shapes interpersonal connections. With greater insight, it becomes possible to foster more empathetic approaches to communication and conflict resolution, ultimately paving the way for healthier and more supportive relational patterns.

Paranoia in Romantic Relationships

Romantic relationships thrive on trust, openness, and mutual understanding—qualities that can be incredibly difficult to achieve when one partner struggles with Paranoid Personality Disorder (PPD). For individuals with PPD, the vulnerability inherent in romantic partnerships often triggers heightened suspicion and fear of betrayal. Seemingly routine occurrences, such as a partner's delayed reply to a message or an innocent interaction with someone else, may be perceived as signs of dishonesty or infidelity. These misinterpretations can lead to excessive questioning, accusations, or even attempts to control the partner's behavior in an effort to feel secure.

The constant presence of mistrust erodes the emotional foundation of the relationship, making it difficult to foster the intimacy that healthy relationships depend on.

Partners of individuals with PPD often find themselves caught in a draining cycle, trying to prove their loyalty and intentions but facing persistent skepticism. Efforts to provide reassurance may be misread or dismissed, further deepening the divide.

This dynamic can create significant emotional strain for both partners. The individual with PPD may feel trapped by their own fears, while their partner may experience frustration, confusion, or sadness as they navigate the challenges of the relationship. Without intervention, this ongoing tension can lead to conflict and emotional distance, weakening the bond over time.

However, despite these difficulties, relationships involving PPD are not without hope. Compassionate communication, where both partners actively listen and express themselves with empathy, can help create a foundation for mutual understanding. Seeking professional support, such as therapy, can provide additional tools for addressing the underlying fears and mistrust that drive the disorder. Through patience and commitment, couples can work toward a more balanced and supportive partnership, even in the presence of PPD.

The Strain of Family and Friendships

Family and friendships play a vital role in providing support and a sense of belonging, but for individuals with Paranoid Personality Disorder (PPD), these relationships are often marked by tension and misunderstanding. The pervasive mistrust associated with PPD can lead individuals to perceive even their closest loved ones as potential threats. They may suspect family members or friends of harboring hidden motives, spreading rumors, or withholding important information, even when no evidence supports these beliefs.

This deep-seated suspicion often results in behaviors that alienate others. Individuals with PPD may avoid social interactions, fearing judgment or betrayal, or they may withhold personal information to protect themselves from perceived harm. These defensive actions can leave family members and friends feeling confused, hurt, or frustrated, as their genuine attempts to connect or reassure are often met with skepticism.

For those trying to maintain relationships with someone living with PPD, the experience can be emotionally taxing. Efforts to bridge the gap may be misinterpreted, leading to further strain. Over time, this cycle of mistrust and defensiveness can erode bonds, leaving the individual with PPD increasingly isolated—a state that often reinforces their belief that others are untrustworthy.

Despite these challenges, meaningful relationships are not impossible. Building or maintaining connections requires patience, empathy, and a willingness to understand the fears underlying the person's behavior. Loved ones can help by creating a stable and non-threatening environment, avoiding actions that might be perceived as intrusive or deceptive, and gently encouraging open communication. While progress may be slow, consistent and compassionate efforts can provide a pathway to rebuilding trust and fostering stronger, more supportive relationships over time.

Trust Issues and Communication Breakdown

Trust issues lie at the heart of many relational struggles faced by individuals with Paranoid Personality Disorder (PPD). The pervasive inability to trust others creates a constant backdrop of suspicion, turning even routine interactions into potential sources of conflict. Communication, which is meant to foster connection and understanding, becomes a minefield of misinterpretation and tension.

For individuals with PPD, simple conversations often feel loaded with hidden agendas. A neutral comment might be dissected for covert criticisms, while an offer of assistance could be seen as an attempt to manipulate or control. This heightened vigilance transforms ordinary interactions into sources of anxiety and defensiveness, making it difficult for others to communicate without inadvertently triggering suspicion.

These challenges can result in frequent misunderstandings and communication breakdowns. The person with PPD may feel attacked or deceived, while those interacting with them might feel frustrated or unfairly judged. This dynamic not only disrupts the flow of communication but also reinforces the individual's mistrust, perpetuating a cycle of suspicion and misinterpretation.

Navigating these issues requires thoughtful and empathetic communication. It is important to remain patient and avoid defensive reactions, even in the face of accusations or mistrust. Consistency in words and actions can play a crucial role in slowly establishing a sense of reliability. Over time, these efforts can help create a foundation for more constructive communication, offering a pathway to rebuilding trust and fostering healthier interactions.

Navigating Conflict with Paranoid Individuals

Navigating conflict with someone who has Paranoid Personality Disorder (PPD) requires patience, emotional awareness, and a carefully measured approach. For individuals with PPD, disagreements are often viewed through a lens of suspicion, and even minor disputes can feel like attacks or betrayals. This heightened sensitivity and defensiveness can cause tensions to escalate quickly, making resolution particularly challenging.

When conflicts arise, it is essential to remain calm and composed, even if the situation becomes emotionally charged. Reacting with anger or defensiveness can exacerbate the individual's mistrust, reinforcing their belief that they are under attack. Instead, focus on maintaining a steady and empathetic tone, emphasizing understanding rather than blame.

Clear communication is critical in these situations. Avoid vague language or phrases that might be open to interpretation, as these can feed into the person's tendency to misread intent. Instead, be direct but gentle, expressing concerns in a way that avoids triggering feelings of judgment or hostility. Reassurance can also play a crucial role in easing defensiveness, though it must be paired with firm and consistent boundaries to prevent misunderstandings from spiraling further.

Another key strategy is de-escalation. Recognize when the conflict is reaching a point where resolution is no longer possible in the moment and step back to allow emotions to settle. This pause can provide an opportunity to revisit the issue with a clearer perspective later, reducing the likelihood of further escalation.

Seeking professional support can be invaluable. Therapists or counselors can offer tailored strategies for managing conflict, creating a safe space for both parties to express their concerns. A professional mediator can also help reframe misunderstandings and foster healthier communication patterns, making it easier to navigate disputes while preserving the relationship.

Impact on Workplace and Social Interactions

The influence of Paranoid Personality Disorder (PPD) extends beyond close personal relationships, affecting both professional environments and broader social interactions. In the workplace, individuals with PPD often struggle with trust issues, perceiving colleagues or supervisors as threats rather than allies. Feedback, even when constructive, may be misinterpreted as personal criticism or evidence of hidden agendas. This perception can hinder effective collaboration, as the individual might resist working in teams, avoid delegating tasks, or refuse to rely on others due to fear of being undermined or taken advantage of. These behaviors can isolate them professionally, limiting opportunities for growth and advancement.

Social settings present similar challenges. Interactions in group settings, such as networking events or casual gatherings, can feel intimidating or unsafe. Those with PPD may decline invitations or remain distant during social engagements, assuming that others harbor negative intentions or judgments. Even seemingly positive gestures, like a compliment or a friendly inquiry, might be scrutinized for hidden motives. This guarded demeanor makes forming meaningful social connections difficult, which can exacerbate feelings of loneliness and reinforce the cycle of mistrust.

Addressing these difficulties requires a multifaceted approach. In professional settings, fostering an environment of transparency, fairness, and respect can help reduce feelings of suspicion. Open communication, clear expectations, and consistent behavior from colleagues and supervisors can create a sense of predictability, which may ease some of the individual's anxiety. In social contexts, providing reassurance and maintaining patience can encourage more positive interactions over time.

For individuals with PPD, therapy offers valuable tools for managing these environments. Cognitive-behavioral therapy, for example, can help challenge distorted thought patterns and develop healthier coping strategies. With time, therapeutic support can empower individuals to engage more comfortably in social and professional settings, ultimately improving their quality of life and sense of belonging.

Paranoid Personality Disorder profoundly affects relationships at every level, from romantic partnerships to workplace dynamics and social connections. The pervasive mistrust and heightened suspicion characteristic of the disorder create barriers to forming and maintaining meaningful relationships, often leading to isolation and conflict. However, understanding the unique struggles faced by individuals with PPD and adopting empathetic, patient, and consistent approaches can help mitigate these challenges. Through professional support, thoughtful communication, and the creation of supportive environments, it is possible to foster healthier connections and provide individuals with PPD the tools they need to thrive.

Chapter 7: Treatment Approaches for Paranoid Personality Disorder

Treating Paranoid Personality Disorder (PPD) necessitates a thoughtful and multi-faceted approach that addresses the disorder's deeply ingrained patterns of mistrust and defensiveness. This pervasive suspicion often makes individuals with PPD hesitant to engage with treatment, as they may question the intentions of healthcare providers or doubt the effectiveness of therapeutic interventions. Overcoming these barriers requires a patient and compassionate strategy, focusing on fostering trust and providing tailored care that acknowledges their unique needs.

The complexity of PPD means that no single treatment is universally effective. Instead, a combination of interventions, adapted to the individual's specific experiences and challenges, often yields the best outcomes. Psychotherapy forms the foundation of treatment, creating a safe space where individuals can begin to explore and challenge their thought patterns. Cognitive Behavioral Therapy (CBT), a widely used modality, offers practical tools for reframing distorted beliefs and improving interpersonal interactions.

In certain cases, medication may be introduced to manage co-occurring symptoms, such as anxiety or depression, that exacerbate the difficulties of PPD. Group therapy, when appropriately timed and facilitated, can provide valuable opportunities for social learning and reinforcement of new skills. Finally, involving family members in the treatment process helps create a supportive network that encourages progress and stability.

This chapter delves into these treatment approaches, highlighting their benefits, limitations, and the careful considerations required for their successful application. By addressing the multifaceted nature of PPD, these methods aim to empower individuals to develop healthier relationships, manage their symptoms more effectively, and lead a more fulfilling life.

Psychotherapy: The Cornerstone of Treatment

Psychotherapy stands as the cornerstone of treatment for Paranoid Personality Disorder (PPD), offering a crucial space for individuals to confront and address the complex emotional and cognitive patterns that define the disorder. One of the primary challenges in therapy for PPD is overcoming the deep-seated mistrust that individuals with this condition often feel toward others. The very idea of therapy can provoke suspicion, as they may question the intentions of the therapist or doubt the efficacy of the therapeutic process. Therefore, establishing a strong, trusting relationship between the therapist and the individual is essential for any meaningful progress.

In the therapeutic environment, the goal is not only to create a safe and nonjudgmental space but also to foster a sense of empathy and understanding. A skilled therapist works to build rapport gradually, allowing the individual to feel more secure in exploring their thoughts, feelings, and anxieties. Given that individuals with PPD are often hypervigilant and defensive, the therapist must be patient and persistent in gaining their trust, demonstrating consistently that the therapeutic environment is one of safety rather than judgment.

Once this trust is established, the focus of therapy shifts to helping individuals recognize and challenge their paranoid thoughts. Many individuals with PPD view the world through a lens of suspicion, interpreting benign actions or words as hostile or manipulative. Through psychotherapy, individuals can learn to identify these distorted thought patterns and work on reframing them in a way that fosters healthier perspectives.

An essential aspect of therapy for PPD is helping individuals understand the impact their mistrust has on their relationships and daily life. Often, people with PPD isolate themselves or push others away due to their fears of betrayal or deceit, and therapy offers a space to examine these behaviors. By fostering insight into the ways in which these fears manifest, individuals can begin to develop more adaptive ways of engaging with others.

The process of change is often slow and gradual, as individuals with PPD typically approach therapy with caution and skepticism. However, the therapeutic relationship itself plays a crucial role in facilitating long-term change. With consistent, empathetic support, individuals can begin to confront their fears, challenge their beliefs, and ultimately improve their interpersonal relationships and overall quality of life.

Cognitive Behavioral Therapy (CBT) and Its Role

Cognitive Behavioral Therapy (CBT) is one of the most effective therapeutic approaches for managing Paranoid Personality Disorder (PPD). Its primary focus is on identifying and altering the distorted thought patterns that contribute to the paranoia and mistrust characteristic of the disorder. Many individuals with PPD develop a tendency to perceive others' actions or intentions as threatening, even when no such threat exists. These cognitive distortions can cause them to misinterpret neutral or innocuous situations as personal affronts or conspiracies.

CBT works by helping individuals with PPD recognize these cognitive biases and teaching them how to challenge and reframe their thoughts. In therapy, the individual might learn to identify automatic thoughts such as, "My coworker didn't greet me today because they're plotting against me," and replace them with a more balanced interpretation, such as, "Maybe they were preoccupied with something or simply didn't notice me." This process of cognitive restructuring helps the individual view situations more realistically, reducing the intensity of their paranoid thoughts.

One of the key elements of CBT is teaching clients to consider alternative explanations for their perceptions. This can be particularly challenging for individuals with PPD, as they often see the world through a lens of suspicion. However, by gradually learning to question their assumptions and consider different perspectives, they can start to develop a more accurate understanding of others' intentions. For instance, they might begin to realize that not every interaction is a potential threat or manipulation, and that most people are not out to harm them.

Beyond cognitive techniques, CBT also incorporates behavioral strategies aimed at breaking the cycle of avoidance and withdrawal that often accompanies PPD. People with PPD tend to avoid social interactions or become defensive in unfamiliar situations, fearing that they will be judged or deceived. Through CBT, individuals are encouraged to gradually engage in social activities and practice healthier ways of interacting with others. These behavioral exercises might include role-playing or real-life exposure to situations that challenge their paranoid thoughts, such as initiating a conversation or attending a social gathering.

As individuals practice these skills in everyday situations, they begin to build confidence and resilience. The more they experience positive interactions and realize that their fears were unfounded, the more their paranoia diminishes. This can lead to a significant reduction in the emotional toll of PPD, allowing individuals to build more authentic relationships and engage with the world in a more balanced and positive way.

In sum, CBT provides individuals with PPD a structured and effective way to address the core cognitive distortions driving their paranoia. By challenging irrational thoughts and gradually exposing themselves to social situations, individuals can gain a clearer understanding of their relationships and develop more adaptive coping strategies. With time and persistence, CBT can play a vital role in helping individuals with PPD lead healthier, more fulfilling lives.

Medication: When and How It Is Used

Medication is not typically the first line of treatment for Paranoid Personality Disorder (PPD), as psychotherapy is generally considered the most effective approach. However, medications can be an important supplementary tool, particularly for managing specific symptoms or addressing co-occurring conditions such as anxiety, depression, or severe mood disturbances. These medications can help alleviate some of the distressing aspects of PPD, making it easier for individuals to engage in therapy and begin working on their underlying issues.

In cases where individuals with PPD experience significant anxiety or tension, anti-anxiety medications such as benzodiazepines or selective serotonin reuptake inhibitors (SSRIs) may be prescribed. These medications can help reduce the chronic feelings of unease and stress that often accompany the disorder, enabling the individual to feel more at ease in therapy and social situations.

For individuals who experience significant mood disturbances, antidepressants can also be useful. Many people with PPD suffer from low self-esteem, depression, or irritability, and medications such as SSRIs or serotonin-norepinephrine reuptake inhibitors (SNRIs) can help stabilize mood and reduce emotional fluctuations. This can create a more stable emotional environment, allowing for more productive therapeutic work and helping to manage the emotional strain that often accompanies the disorder.

In cases where delusional thinking becomes particularly severe—where an individual's paranoia leads to significant distortions of reality, such as believing they are being persecuted or targeted—antipsychotic medications may be considered. These medications can help manage psychotic symptoms by addressing the distorted thoughts and reducing the intensity of delusions. However, antipsychotics are generally used as a last resort and in conjunction with other therapeutic approaches, as they come with potential side effects and are not specifically targeted for PPD.

Despite these benefits, individuals with PPD may be hesitant to take medication. Their pervasive mistrust and suspicion can lead them to fear the intentions of healthcare providers or doubt the effectiveness of prescribed treatments. For these individuals, medication may be viewed as another source of potential betrayal, which can hinder treatment adherence. To overcome these barriers, healthcare providers must take extra care in establishing trust and providing clear, honest explanations about the role of medications in treatment. Building a strong therapeutic alliance is essential to alleviating these concerns, ensuring that the individual understands how the medication works, its potential benefits, and any side effects to expect.

Medication should never be considered a stand-alone treatment for PPD. It is most effective when used as part of a comprehensive treatment plan that includes psychotherapy. In fact, medication can make psychotherapy more effective by reducing the intensity of anxiety or mood fluctuations, allowing individuals to focus on addressing the core issues of their paranoia and mistrust. A holistic approach, combining both medication and therapy, offers the best chance for individuals with PPD to experience lasting improvement in their symptoms and overall quality of life.

The Role of Group Therapy in Healing

Group therapy can be a powerful tool in the treatment of Paranoid Personality Disorder (PPD), offering individuals the opportunity to work on social skills, build trust, and engage with others in a supportive, structured environment. However, it is essential to note that group therapy may not always be suitable in the early stages of treatment due to the deep mistrust and defensiveness common in individuals with PPD. In the initial phases of therapy, individuals may need to focus more on building trust with a therapist in a one-on-one setting before they are ready to engage in group dynamics.

Once individuals have made progress in individual therapy and are more open to social interactions, group therapy can become an invaluable tool. It offers a safe space for practicing interpersonal skills in real-life situations, which can be especially beneficial for those with PPD, as they often struggle with misinterpreting others' intentions and avoiding social interactions. In group settings, participants can role-play and engage in exercises that challenge their assumptions about others, allowing them to test out new behaviors and perceptions.

One of the most significant benefits of group therapy is the opportunity for individuals with PPD to hear from others who may share similar experiences. Listening to the perspectives of fellow group members can provide critical insights into how their paranoid thinking affects relationships and daily interactions. It can also help individuals realize that their experiences and perceptions are not entirely unique, reducing feelings of isolation and reinforcing the idea that they are not alone in their struggles.

Furthermore, witnessing healthy interactions within the group can serve as a model for positive social behavior. Observing others engage in open, honest conversations, express vulnerability, and resolve conflicts in a constructive manner can encourage individuals with PPD to challenge their own patterns of mistrust and defensiveness. Over time, this exposure can help reshape their understanding of social interactions and foster more balanced, trusting relationships.

However, the success of group therapy depends on the skill and experience of the therapist facilitating the sessions. A therapist must be able to manage the complexities of interpersonal dynamics within the group and address any triggers that may arise. In particular, individuals with PPD may find it challenging to navigate the vulnerabilities associated with group therapy, as the interactions may stir up feelings of paranoia or reinforce their existing fears of betrayal. A skilled therapist can help mitigate these challenges by creating a safe, respectful environment where members feel heard and supported.

Additionally, group therapy is most effective when group members are carefully selected. Individuals who are at different stages of their treatment may not be ready to engage in group settings, and certain group dynamics may exacerbate feelings of mistrust. The therapist must ensure that the group is composed of individuals who are capable of engaging in open, non-judgmental interactions. This careful curation can help minimize the risks of triggering paranoid thoughts and promote healing through shared experiences and mutual support.

In summary, group therapy can play a pivotal role in the treatment of PPD, providing individuals with the opportunity to develop social skills, challenge distorted thinking, and build trust in others. When facilitated by a skilled therapist and designed to address the unique challenges of PPD, group therapy can foster personal growth and lead to meaningful improvements in social relationships. However, it is essential to approach group therapy cautiously and consider it as a complement to individual therapy, rather than a replacement.

Integrating Family Support in Treatment

Integrating family support into the treatment of Paranoid Personality Disorder (PPD) is a vital component of the recovery process. Individuals with PPD often direct their mistrust and defensiveness toward those closest to them—family members, in particular. These dynamics can create significant strain, as loved ones may feel helpless or hurt by the constant suspicion and emotional distance. When family members are involved in the therapeutic process, it can lead to a deeper understanding of the disorder and create a more supportive environment for the individual to engage in treatment and work through their challenges.

Family therapy provides a valuable platform for loved ones to voice their concerns, express their feelings, and gain insights into the complexities of PPD. It offers a space where family members can better understand how the individual's paranoia shapes their perceptions and behaviors, and how this affects relationships. This knowledge can significantly reduce the frustration, confusion, and emotional exhaustion that family members often experience when interacting with someone who has PPD. Understanding that the mistrust is rooted in the disorder and not a personal attack on them allows family members to separate the individual's behavior from their own self-worth, leading to a reduction in resentment.

Education plays a key role in empowering family members. By learning about the nature of PPD, family members can better comprehend the challenges their loved one faces. They gain a clearer perspective on how paranoid thoughts and defensiveness manifest in daily life. This knowledge helps reduce misunderstandings and fosters empathy, creating a more supportive and less reactive environment. Families are then able to respond with greater patience and care, avoiding actions or words that may unintentionally trigger feelings of mistrust.

In addition to understanding the disorder, family therapy teaches practical strategies for responding to paranoid behaviors in a constructive manner. Family members can learn how to set healthy boundaries while maintaining compassion. For example, they might practice how to provide reassurance without sounding defensive or dismissive, as individuals with PPD may interpret even neutral or helpful comments as signs of hostility. Therapists can also guide families in maintaining consistency in their interactions, helping to establish a sense of stability and predictability that individuals with PPD need to feel safer in their relationships.

Another crucial aspect of family support is encouraging the individual with PPD to stay engaged in treatment. This might involve gently guiding them to therapy sessions, reminding them of the benefits of treatment, and offering reassurance when they express doubts or fears about the process. The encouragement and active involvement of family members can help individuals with PPD navigate the discomfort and uncertainty they may feel when facing therapy. A strong and understanding support system provides the emotional strength needed to confront the difficult emotions and changes involved in treatment.

Moreover, a stable and caring family environment can enhance the individual's overall well-being, reinforcing the positive changes made in therapy. The family's role in creating a safe and nurturing space contributes to a sense of security that can make a significant difference in recovery. As the individual progresses in therapy, the family's involvement continues to play an essential role in reinforcing healthy behaviors and improving communication, contributing to long-term success.

In conclusion, family support is an indispensable element in the treatment of PPD. When family members are educated about the disorder, understand the behaviors associated with it, and learn strategies to engage in constructive interactions, they can help foster a therapeutic environment that encourages growth and healing. By offering consistent, compassionate support, families contribute to creating a stable foundation for the individual with PPD, enabling them to make meaningful progress in therapy and improve their relationships.

Chapter 8: Cognitive Behavioral Strategies for Managing Paranoia

Paranoid thinking can be deeply disruptive, influencing how individuals interact with others, process daily events, and perceive the world around them. It can lead to heightened anxiety, misinterpretations of innocent actions, and difficulties in trusting others. This chronic state of suspicion can significantly impair an individual's ability to form and maintain healthy relationships, both personally and professionally. It can also hinder overall well-being, making routine tasks feel overwhelming or unsafe.

Fortunately, Cognitive Behavioral Therapy (CBT) provides a powerful, structured framework to help individuals tackle and reduce these paranoid thoughts. CBT is grounded in the idea that thoughts, feelings, and behaviors are interconnected, and by addressing and changing distorted thinking patterns, individuals can experience real, positive changes in their emotions and behaviors. This chapter delves into practical, evidence-based strategies within CBT specifically designed to address paranoia.

By learning to identify and challenge irrational thoughts, individuals can begin to alter their negative cognitive patterns and replace them with more balanced and realistic perspectives. Additionally, CBT emphasizes the development of coping mechanisms to manage anxiety and stress, which often fuel paranoia. Rebuilding trust—both in oneself and in others—is another critical aspect of the therapy, helping individuals move past the pervasive mistrust that defines paranoid thinking.

Finally, the tools discussed in this chapter will help foster healthier cognitive patterns. These techniques empower individuals to regain control over their thought processes, reducing the grip that paranoia holds over their lives. As individuals work through these steps, they can experience more fulfilling relationships, improved emotional regulation, and a stronger sense of self-trust, ultimately leading to a more balanced and secure outlook on life.

Identifying and Challenging Paranoid Thoughts

The first critical step in managing paranoid thinking is recognizing and identifying the specific paranoid thoughts that arise. These thoughts often manifest as an automatic, knee-jerk reaction to everyday interactions, where the individual interprets the actions or intentions of others as malicious or threatening. For example, a person with paranoid thoughts may believe that someone is intentionally avoiding them, spying on them, or conspiring against them without any concrete evidence to support these claims. Often, these thoughts are distorted, forming a cycle of mistrust that can impact personal and professional relationships.

Since paranoid thoughts are typically automatic and triggered by certain situations, it can be difficult for individuals to consciously recognize them as irrational or untrue. They may feel convinced that others are intentionally trying to harm them, even when the actions in question are benign. This is where awareness becomes crucial: taking a step back to observe and pinpoint these thoughts is the first key to breaking the cycle.

Once these paranoid thoughts are identified, the next step is to challenge them. This involves critically examining the evidence that supports the belief and considering alternative, more plausible explanations. For instance, if a person believes that a friend is intentionally ignoring their calls, they can ask themselves: "Is there any reason to believe this is intentional? Could my friend be busy or dealing with personal issues?" By questioning the assumptions that underpin these thoughts, individuals can often find that they are not based on objective facts, but rather on distorted perceptions.

Challenging paranoid thoughts is an essential part of Cognitive Behavioral Therapy (CBT), which helps individuals recognize common cognitive distortions like mind reading (assuming we know what others are thinking), catastrophizing (expecting the worst possible outcome), or personalizing (believing that something negative is about them when it isn't). A therapist can support individuals in this process by guiding them through specific instances where their paranoia may have been triggered and helping them reframe these situations with a more grounded perspective. Over time, this structured approach enables individuals to break free from the cycle of paranoia and begin forming more balanced, realistic views of the world and the people around them.

As individuals practice this process of challenging their paranoid thoughts, they will gradually develop the ability to think more critically and objectively in everyday situations. This shift leads to greater emotional stability and healthier relationships, as the grip of irrational fears loosens and trust in others can begin to be rebuilt.

Coping Skills for Reducing Anxiety and Stress

Paranoia is often closely linked to heightened anxiety and stress, which can create a cycle that reinforces distorted thinking and further erodes a person's sense of control. When anxiety is elevated, the mind tends to amplify irrational fears, making it even more difficult for individuals to distinguish between reality and their paranoid perceptions. To break this cycle, developing effective coping skills is essential. These strategies can help individuals manage their anxiety, regulate stress, and regain clarity in moments of distress.

One powerful tool for managing anxiety is deep breathing. By focusing on slow, deliberate breaths, individuals can activate the body's natural relaxation response, which helps to lower heart rate, reduce blood pressure, and ease muscle tension. Deep breathing exercises, such as diaphragmatic breathing, guide the individual to breathe deeply from the abdomen rather than shallowly from the chest, fostering a state of calmness and focus. When practiced regularly, deep breathing can become a quick and effective tool to counteract anxiety in high-stress situations.

Mindfulness techniques are another key strategy in managing paranoia and anxiety. Mindfulness involves paying attention to the present moment without judgment, helping individuals detach from anxious thoughts about the future or worries over past events. By observing their thoughts and emotions without reacting to them, individuals can create a mental distance from the paranoia, reducing its emotional grip. Regular mindfulness practices, such as focusing on the sensations of breathing or performing body scans, can help individuals stay grounded, preventing them from spiraling into a cycle of irrational thinking.

Progressive muscle relaxation (PMR) is also highly effective in managing stress. This technique involves tensing and relaxing different muscle groups in the body, which encourages a physical release of tension. By focusing on the sensation of relaxation after each muscle group is released, individuals can become more aware of their body's physical state, helping to reduce the physical symptoms of anxiety that accompany paranoia, such as tightness, headaches, or shallow breathing.

Beyond these relaxation techniques, engaging in regular physical activity, such as walking, yoga, or swimming, can have profound effects on reducing stress and anxiety. Exercise triggers the release of endorphins—natural mood boosters—that help to lift spirits and improve overall mental health. It also serves as an outlet for pent-up stress, providing a healthy and constructive way to release negative emotions.

Finally, Cognitive Behavioral Therapy (CBT) encourages individuals to incorporate these physical and mental coping strategies into their daily lives as part of a holistic approach to managing anxiety and stress. By combining relaxation techniques with cognitive reframing, individuals can learn to identify when their anxiety is escalating and use these coping tools to restore balance before their paranoid thoughts take over. Over time, these practices not only help to reduce anxiety but also improve emotional regulation, promoting greater well-being and mental clarity.

Building Healthy Thought Patterns

One of the primary goals of Cognitive Behavioral Therapy (CBT) for managing paranoia is to shift from unhealthy, distorted thought patterns to more balanced, realistic ways of thinking. Cognitive distortions, which are ingrained ways of interpreting experiences, play a central role in reinforcing paranoid beliefs. These patterns often amplify the sense of threat and mistrust, making it harder for individuals to see situations and relationships in a balanced way. Recognizing and challenging these distortions is crucial in fostering a healthier mental state and reducing paranoia.

One common cognitive distortion that individuals with paranoia often experience is black-and-white thinking, also known as all-or-nothing thinking. This occurs when situations, people, or events are seen as entirely good or entirely bad, with no middle ground. For example, a person with paranoia might believe that if someone doesn't respond to a message promptly, they must be ignoring them intentionally or plotting something harmful. This rigid thinking prevents them from recognizing the complexity of human behavior and the many possible explanations for actions. To counter this, CBT encourages the practice of cognitive reframing, which involves consciously looking for alternative explanations. In the example above, the individual might consider that the person could simply be busy or dealing with their own distractions, rather than jumping to the conclusion that they're being ignored or deceived.

Catastrophizing is another prevalent cognitive distortion, where individuals assume the worst possible outcome in every situation. For someone with paranoia, this might manifest as expecting that every minor inconvenience or misunderstanding will lead to disastrous consequences. For instance, if someone overhears a conversation and misinterprets it, they might immediately believe that others are talking about them in a negative way. Instead of letting these thoughts spiral into panic, CBT teaches individuals to pause and ask themselves: *What is the most likely outcome in this situation?* By taking a step back and questioning the evidence for their catastrophic predictions, individuals can start to challenge the belief that the worst-case scenario is the only possibility.

Another helpful technique in building healthier thought patterns is the practice of gathering evidence. This involves evaluating the actual facts of a situation rather than relying on assumptions or feelings. For example, instead of assuming that a colleague is out to get them, the individual could review past interactions for evidence of kindness or neutrality. They might find that their colleague has been supportive, and that their suspicions were unfounded. This process helps individuals gain a more accurate and objective view of reality, which reduces the tendency to project paranoia onto others.

Ultimately, the process of building healthier thought patterns requires time, patience, and consistent practice. Over time, by identifying and challenging cognitive distortions such as black-and-white thinking and catastrophizing, individuals can develop a more nuanced, balanced way of interpreting their experiences. This shift toward healthier thinking not only helps reduce paranoia but also improves emotional resilience, making it easier to navigate social interactions and build trusting relationships. By embracing these cognitive strategies, individuals can regain a greater sense of control over their thoughts, emotions, and behaviors.

The Importance of Thought Journaling

Thought journaling is an incredibly effective tool within Cognitive Behavioral Therapy (CBT) for individuals dealing with paranoia. It serves as a practical method for helping individuals understand and manage their thoughts, offering a structured space to track, reflect on, and challenge paranoid thinking. Writing down thoughts and feelings provides a sense of distance between the individual and their emotions, which can be especially useful when paranoia leads to intense, irrational reactions. By stepping back and reviewing their thoughts, individuals can gain clarity and perspective, allowing them to address the root causes of their paranoia rather than being overwhelmed by it.

When individuals begin journaling, they can start by recording specific situations that trigger their paranoid thoughts. This can include instances where they feel someone is criticizing them, plotting against them, or being deceitful. By writing down these experiences, individuals can begin to observe patterns in their thinking and identify common triggers. Recognizing these patterns is key to understanding how paranoia arises and, eventually, how to interrupt its cycle.

In addition to identifying triggers, journaling allows individuals to document the nature of their thoughts. They can describe the specific paranoid beliefs they hold, such as assuming that someone is intentionally ignoring them or that they are being judged. This step of the process helps bring awareness to the thought itself and the emotional response that follows. Often, these thoughts can feel overwhelming or all-encompassing, but journaling provides a method to separate the individual from their thoughts and emotions, offering more room for reflection and critical thinking.

A crucial part of thought journaling is the evaluation of the evidence for and against the paranoid thoughts. For example, if someone believes that a colleague is deliberately avoiding them, they can write down the facts that support this belief, such as an instance where the colleague didn't respond to a message. Then, they can balance this with alternative, more realistic interpretations, such as the colleague being busy or having personal issues that prevent them from responding promptly. This process of gathering evidence and considering alternative explanations is at the heart of challenging distorted thinking and reframing paranoid thoughts in a more balanced light.

Journaling also encourages the practice of generating alternative, healthier interpretations of situations. Instead of immediately jumping to a conclusion that others are plotting against them, individuals can write down more reasonable alternatives. For instance, rather than interpreting a lack of eye contact as a sign of deceit, they could explore the possibility that the person was simply distracted or uncomfortable. Over time, this practice can help shift thought patterns, fostering a greater sense of calm and balance in responding to perceived threats.

Furthermore, journaling serves as a valuable tool for tracking progress. As individuals continue to journal their thoughts over weeks or months, they can review past entries and reflect on how their thinking has evolved. Seeing how paranoid thoughts have decreased in frequency or intensity can be an important source of motivation. It also reinforces the idea that change is possible, even if it feels gradual. By consistently engaging in thought journaling, individuals gain a deeper understanding of their thought processes and develop greater control over them, which is essential for managing paranoia in the long term.

Ultimately, thought journaling not only helps individuals manage their paranoid thoughts in the moment, but it also empowers them to develop healthier thinking patterns and track their journey toward healing. The practice of writing down thoughts and evaluating them with objectivity and care is a powerful method for reducing emotional reactivity and improving overall mental well-being.

Techniques for Rebuilding Trust

Rebuilding trust is one of the most important and challenging aspects of managing paranoia. For individuals dealing with paranoid thoughts, trust is often in short supply—whether it's trusting others or trusting their own judgments. A deep sense of suspicion and the fear of betrayal can make it difficult to form or maintain relationships. Rebuilding trust, therefore, requires a systematic, patient approach. It's a process that involves unlearning years of deeply ingrained beliefs and feelings, replacing them with healthier and more balanced ways of interacting with the world.

One effective technique for rebuilding trust is to start small, focusing on low-risk, less threatening situations. When someone with paranoia begins to practice trusting, it's important that they take gradual steps. For instance, an individual might begin by sharing a small personal detail with a close friend or asking for a minor favor from someone they trust. These initial experiences can serve as practice runs, where the individual can see firsthand that trust doesn't always lead to betrayal. By experiencing positive interactions in these controlled environments, their belief in the possibility of trust begins to grow.

As trust is slowly rebuilt in these low-stakes situations, individuals can begin to expand their circle of trust. The key here is to focus on situations where the risk of harm is minimal, allowing the person to test the waters of trust without the overwhelming fear of a negative outcome. Each successful instance of trust, no matter how small, is a building block in developing a more positive and secure view of relationships.

Another crucial component of rebuilding trust is to explore the origins of mistrust in therapy. For many individuals with paranoia, their mistrust has deep roots in past experiences or even trauma. By working through these past experiences, they can begin to understand how these events contributed to their current perceptions and fears. A therapist can guide them in identifying patterns that stem from old wounds, allowing them to process their fears more healthily and in a way that doesn't bleed into present-day relationships. Understanding that their paranoid thoughts may have a foundation in past trauma—rather than being an accurate reflection of current reality—can help individuals challenge their mistrust in a compassionate and non-judgmental way.

In addition to exploring past experiences, rebuilding trust also involves learning to trust one's own judgment. This can be particularly difficult for individuals with paranoia, as they may doubt their instincts or feel constantly on guard. However, by learning to differentiate between genuine threats and exaggerated fears, individuals can develop confidence in their ability to assess situations without immediately defaulting to suspicion. This process of learning to trust one's own judgment is crucial in rebuilding self-esteem and fostering a sense of personal empowerment. Individuals can learn to recognize that not every situation is as dangerous or threatening as it initially appears. Over time, this shift allows them to rely on their intuition in a healthier, more balanced way.

A key component of rebuilding trust is recognizing that it is a gradual process. There is no immediate fix, and setbacks are common. Trust isn't something that can be restored overnight, but with consistency, small successes, and therapeutic guidance, it can be rebuilt piece by piece. The important thing is to persist, even when progress feels slow or when old fears resurface. With continued effort, individuals can regain the ability to trust themselves and others, reducing the pervasive feelings of fear and suspicion that accompany paranoia.

As trust is gradually restored, relationships can begin to thrive. People with paranoid thoughts often experience isolation, believing that others will ultimately betray them. But as trust grows, the walls of isolation begin to break down. This leads to healthier, more fulfilling relationships and a significant reduction in the pervasive fear and suspicion that often defines Paranoid Personality Disorder (PPD). Rebuilding trust doesn't just improve relationships with others—it also fosters a more positive and compassionate relationship with oneself.

In conclusion, techniques for rebuilding trust, when used consistently and supported by therapy, can be a transformative part of managing paranoia. Whether through small, manageable steps, addressing past trauma, or learning to trust one's own instincts, these strategies empower individuals to create healthier relationships, reduce feelings of fear, and navigate the world with greater confidence. While rebuilding trust is not a quick process, the steady progress toward greater self-awareness and connection with others is invaluable, helping individuals with PPD lead more fulfilling lives.

Chapter 9: Coping with Paranoid Thoughts in Daily Life

Living with paranoid thoughts can be incredibly challenging, as they often invade daily life, distorting perceptions of reality and making it difficult to trust others or feel secure. These thoughts can color interactions, leading to feelings of isolation, anxiety, and fear. However, it is possible to manage these thoughts and reduce their impact on one's life with the right tools and strategies. By incorporating practical techniques such as mindfulness, grounding exercises, and self-regulation, individuals can begin to navigate their everyday experiences with greater ease and clarity. This chapter delves into these methods, offering concrete ways to handle paranoia as it arises in daily situations.

At the heart of managing paranoia is the ability to engage with the present moment without being overwhelmed by fearful thoughts or suspicions. Mindfulness practices help individuals cultivate this awareness, allowing them to separate their paranoid thoughts from reality and focus on what is happening around them rather than spiraling into anxiety. Alongside mindfulness, grounding techniques provide essential ways to stay connected to the present, redirecting attention away from irrational fears and back into the body and immediate surroundings.

Paranoia often leads to social withdrawal, as individuals may feel unsafe or misunderstood by others. Yet, reconnecting with people in small, manageable ways can break the cycle of isolation and open the door to healthier, more trusting relationships. This chapter will also discuss how individuals can begin to slowly rebuild trust in others and themselves, one step at a time, through positive social interactions and emotional self-care.

Furthermore, establishing healthy boundaries is key to protecting one's mental and emotional well-being. Learning to assert these boundaries confidently and respectfully helps individuals navigate their relationships more securely while also fostering a sense of control and safety. Finally, addressing the deep-seated fears of betrayal or exploitation that often accompany paranoia can pave the way for a greater sense of trust and resilience.

By integrating these approaches into daily life, individuals with paranoid thoughts can gradually reduce their emotional turmoil, strengthen their relationships, and improve their overall quality of life. The journey may take time, but with persistence and practice, these strategies can provide a solid foundation for overcoming the challenges of paranoia.

Practical Tools for Managing Everyday Paranoia

Managing paranoid thoughts in daily life can feel overwhelming, but developing practical tools can help interrupt the cycle of anxiety and mistrust. One effective method is cognitive reframing, which involves identifying and challenging irrational or negative thoughts as they arise. For example, if someone feels like they are being watched or judged, they can pause and ask themselves, "Is there any real evidence to support this belief?" This simple but powerful technique encourages critical thinking, creating a mental distance from the paranoia and allowing the person to assess the situation more objectively.

Another useful tool is thought-stopping, where individuals consciously interrupt their paranoid thoughts by mentally saying "stop" when they start to arise. This technique can be particularly effective when the thoughts feel overwhelming or intrusive. To enhance this method, pairing thought-stopping with deep breathing exercises helps to calm the body's stress response, encouraging a shift in focus from irrational fears back to the present moment. A few deep breaths can slow the heart rate and reduce anxiety, providing immediate relief from the heightened state of alertness that paranoia often triggers.

In addition to these techniques, maintaining a thought log can help individuals track the frequency and intensity of paranoid thoughts. By writing down the situations that triggered these thoughts, individuals can begin to identify patterns or recurring themes. This insight can be powerful for managing paranoia because it allows people to prepare for situations that might provoke these feelings and develop more effective coping strategies in advance. Regularly reviewing the log can also help individuals see progress over time, offering reassurance that the paranoid thoughts are becoming more manageable.

By incorporating these practical tools into daily life, individuals can gradually regain control over their thoughts, reduce the frequency of paranoid thinking, and cultivate a more balanced perspective. These strategies, when practiced consistently, provide a strong foundation for reducing the impact of paranoia on daily functioning and improving emotional well-being.

The Role of Mindfulness and Grounding Techniques

Mindfulness and grounding techniques are invaluable tools for managing paranoia, offering individuals ways to anchor themselves in the present moment and create distance from the anxiety-provoking thoughts that often accompany paranoid thinking. Mindfulness involves observing one's thoughts, feelings, and physical sensations without judgment. This practice encourages individuals to acknowledge paranoid thoughts as they arise, without reacting to them or allowing them to spiral into overwhelming fear or anxiety. By cultivating this non-judgmental awareness, individuals can begin to view their thoughts more objectively, recognizing them as temporary and not necessarily reflective of reality. This perspective helps reduce the power that paranoid thoughts hold over the individual, fostering a sense of calm and control.

In addition to mindfulness, grounding techniques are powerful strategies for staying connected to the present moment when paranoid thoughts feel overwhelming. One effective grounding technique is to focus on the five senses. This practice encourages individuals to pause and actively engage with their surroundings. For example, they might focus on the texture of an object in their hands, the sound of birds chirping outside, or the colors in the room. Engaging with the senses in this way helps redirect attention from internal fears to the external environment, creating a break in the cycle of paranoid thinking.

These sensory grounding techniques can be particularly helpful when paranoia leads to intense emotional reactions or a sense of disconnection from reality. By grounding themselves in the present, individuals can regain a sense of stability and reduce the intensity of their fears. Mindfulness, when practiced regularly, helps individuals build a skill set for staying grounded during stressful situations, making it easier to manage paranoia as it arises. Over time, the consistent practice of mindfulness and grounding techniques can strengthen the individual's ability to stay calm, clear-headed, and focused, even in moments of heightened anxiety or paranoia.

Incorporating mindfulness and grounding into daily life not only provides immediate relief from paranoid thoughts but also helps individuals build resilience over time, making it easier to manage and navigate the challenges of living with paranoia.

Socializing and Overcoming Isolation

Socializing can be one of the most challenging aspects for individuals dealing with paranoia, as the fear of being judged, misunderstood, or betrayed often leads to isolation. However, this withdrawal from social interaction can worsen feelings of loneliness and intensify the cycle of suspicion and distress. It's essential to recognize that isolation, while providing temporary relief, ultimately reinforces negative beliefs and makes it more difficult to trust others. Overcoming isolation involves taking gradual steps toward rebuilding social connections in a safe and supportive environment.

One effective way to start is by engaging in low-pressure social interactions with people who are already trusted, such as close friends, family, or support groups. These initial interactions allow individuals to experience reassurance and validate their understanding of others' intentions, which can help challenge the fear of betrayal or judgment. Engaging in these smaller, familiar settings creates opportunities to practice social skills and test assumptions about others in a non-threatening way.

Additionally, it's important to remember that socializing doesn't always have to involve deep personal conversations or emotional vulnerability. Sometimes, simply being around others in a shared activity or neutral setting can provide the connection needed to counter isolation. Participating in casual activities, like a walk in the park, joining a community event, or engaging in a group hobby, allows individuals to form bonds without the pressure of divulging personal details or exposing themselves to potentially overwhelming emotional interactions. These more casual moments offer a way to ease into socializing and experience a sense of normalcy, fostering comfort in being around others.

The key to breaking through the walls of isolation is practicing social engagement regularly, even in manageable doses. Over time, as individuals experience positive, low-pressure social interactions, their ability to trust others and feel more secure in social situations will grow. These positive experiences serve as evidence that not all interactions will lead to harm or betrayal, helping to counteract the negative thought patterns that fuel paranoia. By consistently testing and challenging these fears in real-life situations, individuals can gradually rebuild trust, strengthen relationships, and regain confidence in their ability to navigate social spaces.

Socializing, when done at a comfortable pace and in a safe environment, can play a significant role in reducing the emotional toll of paranoia and fostering healthier, more supportive relationships. With practice, the fear of judgment or betrayal can lessen, and the individual's sense of connection to others can be restored.

Developing Healthy Boundaries

Developing healthy boundaries is a vital step in managing paranoid thoughts and protecting one's emotional well-being. For individuals experiencing paranoia, boundaries serve as a tool to create a sense of safety and control, which is essential when dealing with the persistent fear of betrayal, exploitation, or being taken advantage of. Boundaries are not about distancing oneself from others or shutting people out; rather, they are about defining what is acceptable and maintaining personal space in a way that supports emotional and mental health.

The first step in establishing healthy boundaries is self-awareness—understanding what feels comfortable, safe, and secure in interactions with others. This could involve recognizing when certain situations, people, or topics trigger paranoid thoughts or stress. For example, an individual might find that sharing too much personal information with someone leads to feelings of vulnerability, or they might feel uncomfortable in crowded social settings. By identifying these discomforts, they can set clear limits that protect their emotional space. This could include deciding not to share sensitive information with acquaintances or limiting the amount of time spent in social settings where they feel overwhelmed.

Once boundaries are identified, the next step is to communicate those boundaries assertively. This means expressing one's needs in a direct, respectful way that maintains personal integrity without feeling guilty or defensive. It may involve saying things like, "I need some time alone to recharge" or "I'm not comfortable discussing that topic right now." Effective communication ensures that others understand one's needs and helps prevent misunderstandings or feelings of violation. By practicing assertiveness, individuals with paranoia can feel more in control of their interactions and reduce the likelihood of feeling overwhelmed or triggered by external stressors.

Respecting these boundaries through self-care is equally important. This means prioritizing one's emotional and mental health by honoring personal limits and ensuring that they are not pushed beyond what feels comfortable. Regularly practicing self-care routines—such as taking time to rest, engaging in activities that promote relaxation, or seeking support when needed—reinforces these boundaries and encourages a healthier relationship with oneself and others.

Developing and maintaining healthy boundaries also helps increase self-esteem. When individuals assert their limits and feel that their emotional well-being is respected, it boosts their confidence and sense of self-worth. Furthermore, boundaries create a sense of control in relationships, reducing feelings of vulnerability and helping to manage the fear of being exploited or betrayed. Over time, this can strengthen the individual's ability to navigate social interactions and relationships without feeling overwhelmed by paranoia.

Ultimately, establishing healthy boundaries is about recognizing one's needs and protecting emotional health while fostering relationships built on respect and understanding. By practicing this self-awareness and assertiveness, individuals with paranoia can feel more secure, reduce anxiety in their interactions, and gradually rebuild trust in themselves and others.

Coping with Fear of Betrayal or Exploitation

The fear of betrayal or exploitation is a profound challenge for many individuals grappling with paranoid thoughts. This fear can be deeply ingrained, often leading to a pervasive sense of mistrust toward others. People with paranoia may find themselves constantly questioning others' intentions, believing that others are scheming to deceive or manipulate them. This fear can isolate individuals, preventing them from forming meaningful connections or fully engaging with others. Coping with this fear requires both emotional resilience and cognitive strategies that address the root causes of the fear, helping individuals regain a sense of security and trust in their relationships.

A key aspect of managing the fear of betrayal is challenging distorted beliefs. This means actively questioning the assumption that others are always out to harm or deceive. One powerful way to do this is by recalling past positive experiences with others—moments when people have acted with kindness, honesty, and integrity. These memories serve as evidence that not all interactions are driven by malicious intent. For instance, if someone fails to meet expectations, instead of assuming ill intent, an individual could remind themselves that such occurrences are often due to simple human error or external factors like stress or busy schedules. This shift in perspective can significantly reduce the intensity of paranoia, allowing individuals to approach situations with a more balanced view.

Another helpful strategy is cognitive reframing, which encourages individuals to re-evaluate their interpretation of others' actions. Instead of jumping to the conclusion that someone is trying to exploit or deceive them, individuals can consider alternative explanations. If a colleague seems to avoid eye contact, for example, they may simply be feeling nervous or distracted, rather than hiding something. Reframing these situations can help create space between the fear and the actual situation, offering a more objective perspective that decreases the power of the paranoia.

Emotional management is just as crucial in overcoming the fear of betrayal. Practicing self-compassion is an important tool for managing the anxiety that fuels paranoid thoughts. Individuals often judge themselves harshly when they experience fear, believing that their emotions are irrational or unjustified. By learning to treat themselves with kindness, individuals can reduce the shame and guilt that often accompany paranoid thinking. Self-compassion helps to normalize the fear and accept it as part of the human experience, without letting it control actions or beliefs. By acknowledging that fear is a symptom of paranoia and not an accurate reflection of reality, individuals can begin to lessen the emotional grip of fear.

Trust is another critical element in managing paranoia. Rebuilding trust, especially after past betrayals, can take time and requires gradual vulnerability. It's essential to start with small, manageable interactions that allow the individual to test trust without feeling overwhelmed. For instance, trusting a close friend with a small favor or being open about a minor personal issue can serve as stepping stones toward deeper vulnerability. Each successful, positive interaction can slowly replace the fear with a sense of security, reinforcing that not everyone is out to harm them. Over time, these small steps help rebuild trust in others, reducing the emotional toll that the fear of betrayal has on daily life.

One effective way to rebuild trust is to create safe spaces where individuals can feel secure and supported. These spaces could be with trusted friends, family, or even in a therapy setting. Being in environments that are nurturing and nonjudgmental allows individuals to experience vulnerability in a way that feels safe. This can be particularly helpful for managing the fear of being exploited. It's important to remember that vulnerability is not a weakness, but rather a sign of strength and trust in oneself and others.

Finally, practical coping strategies such as setting healthy boundaries, engaging in relaxation techniques, and practicing mindfulness can further help manage the fear of betrayal. By learning to set limits in interactions with others, individuals can feel more in control and less at the mercy of their fears. Grounding techniques like deep breathing and mindfulness help regulate the anxiety that often accompanies these fears, allowing individuals to remain calm and centered in the face of overwhelming thoughts.

Living with paranoid thoughts, especially the fear of betrayal or exploitation, can feel isolating and overwhelming. However, by developing a toolkit of coping strategies, individuals can take significant steps toward reducing the impact of these fears on their lives. Challenging distorted beliefs, practicing self-compassion, reframing situations, and gradually rebuilding trust are all vital components of this process. Though the journey to overcoming paranoia can be slow and requires patience, it is possible to regain control over one's thoughts, emotions, and relationships. With persistence and support, individuals can experience a more balanced, trusting, and fulfilling life.

Chapter 10: The Impact of Paranoid Personality Disorder on Work and Career

Living with Paranoid Personality Disorder (PPD) can have a profound impact on a person's professional life, often leading to challenges in communication, collaboration, and job performance. Paranoia can shape an individual's perceptions, leading them to mistrust colleagues, misinterpret neutral comments or actions, and create unnecessary conflict in the workplace. These patterns not only strain work relationships but can also hinder career growth and job satisfaction. Nevertheless, by recognizing the signs of paranoia, implementing self-regulation techniques, and seeking support when needed, individuals with PPD can take proactive steps to manage their symptoms and succeed in their careers.

The workplace is often a challenging environment for individuals with PPD, as it involves frequent interactions with others and expectations for teamwork, communication, and collaboration. The constant anxiety about being judged, misunderstood, or betrayed can make even everyday tasks feel overwhelming. However, with the right strategies, it is possible to reduce the negative impact of paranoid thoughts and behavior on work life. The following sections will delve into practical strategies for recognizing paranoia in the workplace, navigating work relationships with greater ease, handling the challenges of job searching, improving communication skills, and ultimately finding a balance between mental health and career ambitions. With awareness and intentional effort, individuals with PPD can regain control over their professional lives, foster healthier work environments, and maintain a positive outlook on their career journey.

Recognizing Paranoia in the Workplace

In the workplace, paranoia can manifest in various ways, often affecting both interpersonal dynamics and job performance. Individuals with Paranoid Personality Disorder (PPD) may find themselves suspicious of colleagues, believing that others are plotting against them or speaking negatively behind their back. These suspicions can lead to a constant state of vigilance, where the individual is on high alert, scanning every interaction for signs of betrayal or deceit. For example, a simple comment from a coworker may be misinterpreted as a personal attack or criticism, even if no harmful intent is present. This heightened sensitivity can result in unnecessary conflict, as the individual may react defensively or withdraw from others.

Additionally, paranoia can create challenges in teamwork and collaboration. The fear that others might undermine their efforts can make it difficult for individuals with PPD to trust their colleagues or engage in cooperative work. This mistrust can lead to poor communication, difficulty sharing information, and reluctance to delegate tasks, which can negatively impact group projects and productivity.

The impact of paranoid thinking on job performance can also be significant. When consumed by suspicion, individuals may struggle to concentrate on their work, leading to mistakes or missed deadlines. The tendency to overanalyze situations can also create indecisiveness, as they may second-guess their actions or decisions, fearing they have made a mistake or overlooked a hidden agenda. Furthermore, paranoid thoughts about authority figures can hinder the ability to accept feedback, follow directives, or comply with organizational policies, all of which are critical to professional success.

Recognizing these signs early is essential for individuals with PPD to take proactive steps to manage their symptoms. Awareness of these tendencies allows individuals to seek support from mental health professionals or develop strategies to cope with paranoia in the workplace before it becomes more disruptive. By acknowledging these challenges, individuals can begin to work on shifting their mindset and adopt techniques to maintain a healthier relationship with both themselves and their colleagues.

Strategies for Navigating Work Relationships

Navigating work relationships with Paranoid Personality Disorder (PPD) can be daunting, but with the right strategies, individuals can foster positive connections and create a healthier work environment. One of the most important strategies is effective communication. Open and transparent communication helps to prevent misunderstandings and allows individuals to address concerns before they escalate. For instance, if an employee with PPD feels uneasy about a colleague's actions or words, they can approach the situation by calmly discussing their feelings. Rather than assuming negative intent, they can ask questions or seek clarification, which can often dispel the fear of being judged or targeted. This proactive communication, when done respectfully, can help establish clearer boundaries and prevent unnecessary conflicts.

Setting boundaries is another crucial strategy for managing paranoia in the workplace. While it's important to build professional relationships, individuals with PPD may find it helpful to define and communicate their limits in a way that protects their emotional well-being. For example, during office gatherings or team lunches, if they feel overwhelmed by the social demands, it's perfectly acceptable to politely decline or limit their participation. Setting such boundaries ensures that they maintain a sense of control over their environment, which can reduce feelings of vulnerability and exploitation. By setting personal limits while still participating in work activities, individuals with PPD can strike a balance that supports their mental health.

Another valuable approach is seeking guidance from a trusted mentor, HR representative, or colleague. A neutral party can offer objective perspectives on any concerns and provide constructive advice for managing complex work dynamics. These conversations can also create a safe space to discuss feelings of mistrust and explore ways to address those fears within a professional context. Additionally, working with a therapist or coach can be incredibly beneficial. Therapy or coaching programs focused on improving emotional intelligence and interpersonal skills can provide tailored strategies

for managing paranoia in work relationships. These sessions can help individuals with PPD develop greater self-awareness, enhance communication skills, and build healthier professional connections.

By practicing these strategies—effective communication, setting boundaries, seeking support, and improving interpersonal skills—individuals with paranoia can foster a more supportive and less stressful work environment, improving both their professional relationships and overall job satisfaction.

Managing Paranoia While Job Searching

Managing paranoia during the job search process can be particularly overwhelming for individuals with Paranoid Personality Disorder (PPD), as the uncertainty of the process can amplify feelings of mistrust, fear of rejection, and anxiety. These emotions often make it challenging to feel confident or authentic in interviews and interactions with potential employers. However, with a combination of preparation, cognitive strategies, and finding the right environment, individuals with PPD can navigate this process more effectively and reduce the impact of their paranoia.

Preparation is one of the most effective tools for managing job search anxiety. By practicing common interview questions with a trusted friend, family member, or career coach, individuals can familiarize themselves with the process and alleviate some of the uncertainty. Practicing responses helps build confidence, allowing candidates to focus less on their fears and more on articulating their qualifications. It's also essential to remember that an employer's decision to hire or reject someone often depends on numerous factors, such as the needs of the organization or the suitability of the candidate's experience, and is rarely a reflection of their personal worth. Understanding that rejection is not a personal attack can help reframe feelings of failure and reduce the emotional weight of the process.

Reframing negative thoughts plays a crucial role in managing anxiety during job searches. When feelings of fear, self-doubt, or paranoia arise, individuals can counteract these thoughts by focusing on their strengths, accomplishments, and the positive feedback they've received in past roles. Keeping a journal of achievements, compliments from colleagues or supervisors, and moments of success can provide valuable reminders of their capabilities, helping to restore self-esteem. By shifting the focus away from perceived personal shortcomings, individuals can create a more balanced and realistic self-assessment.

In addition to these strategies, it's essential to seek supportive environments during the job search. When looking for potential employers, individuals with PPD may benefit from targeting companies that are known for prioritizing mental health and offering support resources for employees. Researching a company's culture, reviewing employee testimonials, and reaching out to current or former staff to ask about their experiences can provide valuable insights. Additionally, seeking out roles that offer more flexibility or autonomy, such as remote work or positions with fewer social demands, can make the work environment feel safer and more manageable. This approach allows individuals to find a position that better suits their mental health needs while still advancing in their careers.

By combining thoughtful preparation, reframing negative thoughts, and seeking a supportive workplace, individuals with paranoia can successfully manage the stress of job searching. With these tools, the job search process becomes less about fear and rejection and more about finding a role that aligns with both professional goals and personal well-being.

Enhancing Workplace Communication Skills

Effective communication is essential for success in any workplace, but for individuals with paranoia, it can present unique challenges. Paranoid thoughts often lead to misunderstandings, misinterpretations, and suspicions about colleagues' motives. These feelings can create barriers to open communication, resulting in conflict or strained relationships. However, with focused effort and strategic communication techniques, individuals with paranoia can improve their communication skills and foster healthier work interactions.

One of the most valuable communication strategies is active listening. When individuals with paranoia focus on truly understanding the speaker's perspective, they reduce the likelihood of misinterpreting words or actions. Active listening involves giving full attention to the speaker, maintaining eye contact, and showing empathy through verbal and non-verbal cues. By practicing this skill, individuals can be more present in conversations, allowing them to process information more accurately and reduce the tendency to assume negative intentions. This approach helps prevent knee-jerk reactions and defensive responses, which can escalate misunderstandings.

Another key aspect of improving communication is the willingness to ask for clarification. When something feels ambiguous or causes uncertainty, it's essential to ask questions rather than jumping to conclusions. For example, if a colleague's comment feels critical or dismissive, asking for clarification can help reveal whether it was truly intended that way or if there was a misunderstanding. Approaching conversations with curiosity rather than suspicion opens up the possibility for a clearer, more balanced perspective and prevents assumptions from clouding judgment. When questions are asked politely and with the intention of understanding, individuals can address potential concerns before they evolve into larger issues.

Nonverbal communication plays a significant role in workplace interactions as well. For individuals with paranoia, being attuned to body language, facial expressions, and tone of voice can help them better interpret the emotions and intentions behind the words being spoken. It's equally important to be mindful of their own nonverbal cues, as these can signal defensiveness or discomfort, potentially triggering misunderstandings. Maintaining an open posture, smiling, and using relaxed facial expressions can promote a sense of approachability and collaboration, helping to foster trust with colleagues.

By adopting active listening, seeking clarification, and becoming more attuned to nonverbal signals, individuals with paranoia can enhance their workplace communication skills. These strategies reduce the risk of unnecessary conflicts, improve interactions, and promote a more positive and cooperative work environment. Through consistent practice, individuals can strengthen their ability to engage with others in a constructive, open manner, ultimately contributing to professional success and a more supportive work atmosphere.

Balancing Professional Life with Mental Health

Balancing professional life with mental health is especially important for individuals with Paranoid Personality Disorder (PPD), as the stress of managing paranoid thoughts can take a significant toll on overall well-being. The constant vigilance and hyperawareness of potential threats in the workplace can lead to burnout, anxiety, and emotional exhaustion. In order to succeed professionally and maintain mental health, it is essential to integrate self-care practices, stress management techniques, and a balanced approach to work.

One of the key strategies in maintaining this balance is setting realistic expectations. People with paranoia often struggle with perfectionism or fear of failure, which can lead them to take on excessive work or feel the need to overperform in order to avoid judgment. This tendency to overcommit can quickly result in fatigue and heightened anxiety. It's important for individuals to recognize when they are taking on too much and learn to say no or delegate tasks as needed. Setting boundaries around workload—whether that means limiting the number of tasks or creating a daily structure—helps maintain mental clarity and reduces the likelihood of becoming overwhelmed.

Taking regular breaks throughout the workday is also essential for managing mental health. Stepping away from the desk, going for a walk, or engaging in a quick mindfulness exercise can allow the mind to reset and recharge. Additionally, incorporating moments of relaxation and self-care into daily life can significantly reduce the emotional strain of paranoia. This might involve practicing a hobby, spending time in nature, or connecting with supportive friends and family. Scheduling these breaks and downtime can ensure that mental health is prioritized, preventing the negative effects of continuous stress.

Stress management is another critical component in maintaining a healthy work-life balance. Simple techniques like deep breathing, meditation, or yoga can be powerful tools for reducing the intensity of paranoid thoughts. Even just a few minutes of focused breathing can calm the nervous system and provide relief from anxiety. Regular physical activity, whether through walking, exercising, or engaging in sports, also plays a vital role in lowering stress and improving overall mood. These practices not only help alleviate the symptoms of paranoia but also support long-term emotional and physical health.

Seeking professional support is a crucial element in managing the impact of PPD in the workplace. Therapy, particularly Cognitive Behavioral Therapy (CBT), can be an effective way to challenge paranoid thoughts and develop healthier thinking patterns. A therapist can also help individuals build coping strategies to manage the stress of workplace dynamics and improve interpersonal relationships. Therapy provides a safe space for individuals to discuss their fears and gain insights into how they can navigate work challenges while managing their mental health. Counseling and support groups can also offer opportunities to connect with others facing similar struggles and provide guidance on how to build resilience and coping mechanisms.

By taking a proactive approach to managing mental health, individuals with PPD can improve their ability to handle work pressures while maintaining emotional well-being. Balancing professional life with mental health is not about avoiding challenges but learning to manage them effectively. It requires consistent effort, self-awareness, and a willingness to seek support. With the right strategies in place, individuals can navigate the complexities of work life, manage their paranoid thoughts, and create a more fulfilling and sustainable career. Prioritizing mental health, setting boundaries, and engaging in self-care are vital steps toward a successful and balanced professional life.

Chapter 11: Thriving Beyond Paranoia

Living with Paranoid Personality Disorder (PPD) can often lead to feelings of isolation, fear, and misunderstanding, making it seem like the world is against you. It may feel as though paranoia shapes every interaction, thought, and decision, but the truth is, it doesn't have to define your entire life. Moving beyond paranoia is not about erasing the disorder, but about finding ways to grow, heal, and create a life filled with meaning and purpose. Thriving with PPD involves recognizing that, while paranoia can be a part of your experience, it doesn't have to be the controlling factor in your life.

Embracing personal growth is a key part of thriving with PPD. This means understanding that change is possible, and taking steps to improve your emotional well-being, build stronger relationships, and find purpose in life. Seeking support, whether from loved ones, professionals, or support groups, plays a crucial role in this process. Supportive people can offer guidance, perspective, and encouragement, which can help combat the feelings of suspicion and isolation that often accompany paranoia.

Cultivating emotional resilience is another essential step. Resilience is the ability to bounce back from difficulties and continue moving forward despite setbacks. For those with PPD, emotional resilience means learning to recognize and manage paranoid thoughts, developing healthier coping strategies, and gradually overcoming fears that limit personal growth. It's about acknowledging the presence of paranoia but not allowing it to control your actions or limit your potential.

This chapter delves into the strategies that can help individuals with PPD build a supportive network, find meaning beyond their paranoia, develop emotional resilience, and turn their experiences into strengths. We will explore how to transform what may feel like a barrier to success into a foundation for long-term growth. By focusing on personal strengths, setting achievable goals, and practicing self-compassion, individuals with PPD can begin to reclaim control of their lives and move toward a future where their experiences do not dictate their potential for happiness and fulfillment.

Building a Support System: The Role of Loved Ones

Overcoming the challenges of Paranoid Personality Disorder (PPD) requires more than just self-awareness and coping strategies—it also involves building a reliable, understanding support system. The presence of supportive individuals, such as family, friends, and partners, can make a significant difference in navigating the complexities of paranoia. These people offer much-needed emotional comfort, reassurance, and a sense of connection, which can help counter feelings of isolation that often accompany PPD.

Building a support system begins with identifying people who are trustworthy, empathetic, and patient. These individuals should be the kind of people who are willing to listen attentively without rushing to judgment, offering comfort and encouragement when paranoid thoughts arise. Having someone to talk to, especially during moments of heightened suspicion or anxiety, can provide grounding and perspective. It's not about having a large number of people around but having those who truly understand, care, and are committed to offering support.

For the person living with paranoia, open communication is essential. Sharing the specific challenges and experiences of living with PPD helps those in the support system better understand the nature of paranoia and how it affects one's thoughts and emotions. Educating loved ones about the disorder can prevent misunderstandings and guide them in responding with empathy rather than reinforcing negative patterns.

When loved ones are well-informed, they are better equipped to offer the right kind of support, whether that's reassuring someone when doubts arise or helping them reframe unrealistic fears.

A support system doesn't solely need to consist of family and friends. Seeking help from mental health professionals or support groups can be extremely beneficial. Therapists or counselors can provide an objective, nonjudgmental space to express emotions and explore the root causes of paranoid thoughts. Mental health professionals can also offer practical strategies for managing paranoia and improving coping skills. Additionally, joining support groups with others who understand the challenges of PPD can foster a sense of community and help individuals feel less alone.

The strength of a support system lies in its ability to offer stability and reassurance. It's a safe place where individuals with paranoia can turn to when they need grounding, guidance, or simply a compassionate ear. Over time, these support networks become invaluable in managing the symptoms of PPD, and they help to reduce the feelings of isolation and mistrust that often accompany the disorder. A solid support system not only helps individuals cope with their paranoia but also empowers them to thrive and lead a more connected, fulfilling life.

Finding Purpose and Meaning Beyond Paranoia

One of the most empowering ways to move beyond paranoia is by discovering a sense of purpose that extends beyond the confines of the disorder. When individuals engage in activities that bring personal fulfillment—whether through their careers, hobbies, or community involvement—they begin to focus on their strengths and potential, rather than being consumed by their fears. A sense of purpose provides not only motivation but also a reason to push forward, helping to reshape life's challenges into opportunities for growth and self-discovery.

Pursuing meaningful goals can be a powerful way to shift focus away from paranoia. Whether it's progressing in a career, giving back to a cause, or mastering a new skill, these pursuits foster a deep sense of accomplishment and satisfaction. They offer individuals the opportunity to direct their energy toward positive, tangible outcomes, which can build confidence and a sense of control over their lives. Finding purpose doesn't require grand gestures or radical changes—it can begin with small, purposeful actions that align with one's core values, interests, and passions. Each step forward, no matter how small, can contribute to an evolving sense of fulfillment.

It's also important to recognize that a sense of purpose can be fluid and dynamic, changing over time as life circumstances evolve. What brought meaning to life in one phase may no longer hold the same weight in another. This is completely natural, and embracing this fluidity allows individuals to stay open to new possibilities and redefine their goals as they continue to grow beyond the confines of paranoia.

Allowing room for flexibility in the pursuit of purpose encourages individuals to remain open to new opportunities, build new relationships, and refine their sense of meaning as they evolve. This process of reinvention and discovery can help shift the narrative from one defined by fear and suspicion to one marked by strength, growth, and the pursuit of what truly matters. With time, this sense of purpose can become a powerful tool for overcoming the challenges posed by paranoia, allowing individuals to live a life that is rich in meaning and fulfillment.

Developing Emotional Resilience and Self-Awareness

Emotional resilience is the ability to recover from difficulties, adapt to adversity, and maintain mental well-being. For those living with Paranoid Personality Disorder (PPD), building emotional resilience is particularly important for navigating life's challenges and minimizing the influence of paranoid thoughts. It's about equipping oneself with the tools to not only survive moments of distress but to thrive despite them.

One of the most effective ways to foster emotional resilience is through self-awareness. This involves becoming more attuned to how paranoia influences one's thoughts, feelings, and behaviors. By identifying the patterns of paranoia, individuals can gain greater control over their reactions and take proactive steps to interrupt harmful thought cycles before they spiral out of control. Recognizing that paranoid thoughts are just that—thoughts, and not absolute truths—can be empowering in reducing their grip on daily life.

Mindfulness and self-reflection are valuable practices for enhancing self-awareness and emotional regulation. When paranoid thoughts arise, instead of reacting impulsively or spiraling into anxiety, individuals can pause and acknowledge the thought without judgment.

This pause creates a space to respond thoughtfully rather than emotionally. Over time, this practice strengthens the ability to manage intense emotions and makes it easier to navigate difficult situations with a calm, grounded perspective.

Incorporating regular self-care into one's routine is also crucial for building emotional resilience. Activities that promote physical and mental health—such as regular exercise, eating nourishing foods, and engaging in relaxation techniques like deep breathing or meditation—help reduce stress and improve overall well-being. When the body is cared for, the mind can better cope with emotional turmoil. Additionally, making self-care a priority fosters a sense of control, which is especially important for those who feel vulnerable to external threats.

An important component of resilience is learning to embrace vulnerability. For individuals with paranoia, vulnerability may feel like a weakness or something to avoid, but when reframed as a strength, it can become an essential tool for growth. Being vulnerable means allowing oneself to connect with others more deeply, asking for help when necessary, and expressing emotions without fear of judgment. Vulnerability also opens the door to greater emotional freedom, allowing individuals to experience life more authentically and without the burden of constant suspicion.

By embracing vulnerability and reframing challenges as opportunities for growth, individuals can shift their mindset from one of fear to one of empowerment. Each difficult situation becomes a chance to build resilience and strengthen emotional muscles. Over time, individuals with PPD can develop a more balanced perspective on life, viewing challenges as stepping stones to personal growth rather than insurmountable obstacles. This shift can ultimately help reduce the hold of paranoia and foster a more fulfilling, resilient life.

Transforming Paranoia into Personal Strength

While paranoia can be a challenging and often painful experience, it also holds the potential to be transformed into a personal strength. The heightened vigilance and acute awareness that often accompany paranoia can be reframed as valuable traits, leading to improved skills such as attention to detail, critical thinking, and problem-solving. Individuals with paranoia may develop an increased sensitivity to potential risks or threats, but this sensitivity, when channeled positively, can be a powerful asset in navigating both personal and professional challenges.

Rather than allowing paranoia to dictate fear or anxiety, individuals can learn to use their heightened awareness for self-protection and foresight. For instance, the natural tendency to question intentions or scrutinize situations can be redirected toward making more informed, thoughtful decisions. When faced with a choice, the caution that paranoia often brings can encourage individuals to carefully weigh the pros and cons, ensuring that decisions are made with greater insight and understanding. This level of attention to detail can be especially useful in high-stakes environments where risks need to be assessed thoroughly.

This heightened vigilance can also cultivate a stronger sense of intuition. Individuals may become better at recognizing when something doesn't feel right or when a situation warrants extra caution. Instead of viewing these instincts as irrational or unwarranted, individuals can learn to trust their intuition, using it as a guide to navigate uncertainties in their personal and professional lives.

Moreover, the experiences of paranoia often lead to a deepened empathy for others who feel misunderstood or marginalized. Individuals who have struggled with the challenges of paranoia can often relate to others who face similar feelings of isolation or alienation. This empathy can serve as a foundation for building strong, supportive relationships and engaging in meaningful work that promotes mental health awareness. By using their personal experiences to connect with and support others, individuals can create a sense of community and belonging, transforming their struggles into a source of strength and resilience.

Ultimately, transforming paranoia into personal strength is about shifting the perspective from viewing it as a weakness to recognizing it as a powerful tool for self-growth and understanding. With the right mindset, the very traits that may seem like obstacles can be harnessed to create a more empowered and fulfilling life. Through self-awareness, empathy, and intuition, individuals can turn their challenges into sources of resilience, fostering personal growth and making meaningful contributions to the world around them.

Setting Realistic Goals for Long-Term Growth

Setting realistic, attainable goals is crucial for fostering long-term personal growth and success, especially for individuals with paranoia. When individuals with paranoia create goals, they gain a clearer sense of direction, which helps reduce feelings of uncertainty or helplessness. The process of goal-setting provides a roadmap for moving forward, offering a sense of control and purpose. However, it's important to ensure that the goals set are both achievable and aligned with personal values. Unrealistically high expectations can lead to feelings of failure and frustration, while goals that are too small may feel insignificant and unmotivating.

A key strategy for setting realistic goals is to break them down into smaller, manageable steps. For example, rather than setting an overwhelming, broad goal like "overcome paranoia," it's more effective to focus on specific, incremental actions. These might include goals like "practice mindfulness for five minutes each day," or "initiate one conversation with a colleague without feeling overly anxious." These smaller, more attainable objectives allow individuals to track their progress and celebrate small victories along the way. Achieving these goals creates a sense of accomplishment, which in turn builds confidence and momentum toward larger goals.

It's also important to remain flexible when setting goals. Life is often unpredictable, and circumstances may change, requiring adjustments to one's objectives. Being open to revising goals as needed helps prevent discouragement in the face of setbacks or challenges. For instance, if a certain goal feels too daunting or if external circumstances make it difficult to achieve, adjusting it or breaking it into even smaller steps can help keep the process moving forward. Regularly reviewing and reassessing goals allows individuals to stay focused on progress rather than perfection, ensuring that the path to growth remains sustainable and motivating.

Tracking progress is another important aspect of setting realistic goals. Keeping a journal or progress tracker can help individuals see how far they've come and reinforce a sense of achievement. Reflecting on what's been accomplished, no matter how small, can provide positive reinforcement and help maintain the drive to continue working toward personal growth. These moments of reflection allow individuals to see the bigger picture of their journey, where each step is part of a broader process of healing and self-improvement.

Ultimately, by setting realistic, flexible goals, individuals with paranoia can pave a path toward long-term growth and fulfillment. These goals create a sense of purpose, helping individuals focus on what they can control while minimizing the impact of paranoia. The process of working toward these goals can offer a sense of empowerment, building confidence and resilience that allows individuals to embrace a brighter future, free from the constraints of their fears.

Chapter 12: The Role of Technology in Understanding and Managing PPD

In today's digital world, technology plays a transformative role in mental health care, offering unprecedented opportunities for individuals to manage and understand mental health conditions, including Paranoid Personality Disorder (PPD). Gone are the days when individuals had to rely solely on traditional, in-person visits to therapists or support groups. Now, through the power of technology, a vast range of resources are available at the fingertips of those seeking support and guidance.

The advent of the internet and mobile apps has revolutionized the way mental health services are delivered, making them more accessible, flexible, and often more affordable. For individuals with PPD, technology offers a variety of tools that can assist in managing the symptoms of paranoia, improving self-awareness, and building effective coping mechanisms. From digital therapy sessions that provide privacy and comfort to educational platforms that offer insights into PPD, technology is now an integral part of the healing process.

Furthermore, technology is breaking down the stigma surrounding mental health. Online forums, virtual support groups, and social media platforms allow people to connect with others who share similar experiences. These digital spaces provide a sense of community and understanding, helping individuals with PPD feel less isolated and more empowered to seek help. Virtual therapy and counseling services allow people to access professional care, regardless of geographical barriers, which is especially crucial for those who may find it difficult to engage with traditional in-person services.

As the digital landscape continues to evolve, so too do the tools available to individuals with PPD. This chapter delves into how these technological advancements are shaping mental health care, exploring online resources, digital therapy options, virtual support networks, and a variety of apps designed to help manage paranoia and anxiety. By embracing these tools, individuals with PPD can gain a deeper understanding of their condition, develop essential coping strategies, and take an active role in their journey toward healing and personal growth.

Online Resources and Digital Therapy Options

The internet has opened up an entirely new realm of possibilities for individuals seeking information and support for mental health conditions like Paranoid Personality Disorder (PPD). With just a few clicks, people can access a wealth of knowledge on the nature of PPD, how it affects behavior, and strategies for managing paranoia. Online resources such as dedicated websites, blogs, and forums serve as valuable educational tools, offering insights into the symptoms of PPD and providing advice on how to cope with its challenges. These platforms often feature content created by mental health professionals, providing up-to-date information on treatment options, self-help strategies, and stories from others who share similar experiences.

For individuals with PPD, the anonymity and privacy offered by these digital platforms can make them more approachable and comfortable than traditional methods of seeking help. Many online resources provide interactive content like quizzes, videos, and webinars, allowing individuals to explore and understand their condition at their own pace. Engaging with such resources can help demystify the experience of living with paranoia, making it easier to identify symptoms and access effective coping techniques.

Alongside educational resources, digital therapy options such as teletherapy and online counseling have become increasingly popular. These virtual therapy sessions offer a convenient and flexible way for individuals with PPD to access mental health care without having to leave their homes. For many, this remote access is invaluable, as it removes the barriers of commuting and the potential discomfort of face-to-face interactions. Teletherapy has proven to be effective for various mental health issues, including anxiety, depression, and personality disorders, and many therapists now specialize in online therapy, making it easier to find someone well-suited to the unique challenges of PPD.

Moreover, the flexibility that online therapy platforms offer is a key advantage. Individuals can often schedule sessions during times that suit their lifestyle, whether it's after work or during a lunch break, helping to integrate mental health care into their daily routine. Many of these platforms also provide a range of therapy types, including cognitive-behavioral therapy (CBT), which is commonly used to treat paranoia, as well as more specialized therapy options that cater specifically to personality disorders. For individuals with PPD, the ability to access targeted therapeutic support from the comfort of home can significantly improve their willingness to seek help and commit to treatment.

The anonymity provided by digital therapy options also helps to alleviate some of the stigma that may prevent people from seeking professional help. The privacy of online platforms encourages individuals who may feel self-conscious or ashamed about their mental health struggles to reach out for support without fear of judgment. This increased accessibility, privacy, and flexibility make digital therapy a valuable option for those with PPD, providing an important tool for managing symptoms and improving overall mental well-being.

How Technology Can Aid in Self-Reflection

Self-reflection plays a pivotal role in managing Paranoid Personality Disorder (PPD), as it helps individuals become more aware of their thoughts, emotions, and behaviors. Technology offers an array of tools that can make the process of self-reflection more accessible, structured, and effective. Digital platforms like mood tracking apps and journaling tools provide individuals with an easy way to log their emotions, track shifts in mood, and monitor the onset of paranoid thoughts. This daily practice allows users to recognize patterns in their behavior and emotional responses, which can be especially valuable for those with PPD, as they may often struggle to identify the triggers or root causes of their paranoia. By tracking these patterns over time, individuals can gain a clearer picture of how paranoia manifests in their lives and identify moments when their thoughts may be skewed by irrational fears.

Additionally, apps designed to implement cognitive behavioral therapy (CBT) techniques can offer practical tools for individuals to engage in structured self-reflection. These apps often feature exercises that guide users through challenging irrational thoughts and replacing them with more balanced perspectives. By presenting prompts that encourage users to evaluate their beliefs, analyze their emotional reactions, and challenge distorted thinking, these tools can help individuals build stronger mental habits. For example, an individual might be prompted to question the evidence for a suspicious thought or to identify an alternative, less threatening explanation for a situation. Over time, these exercises can help individuals shift from harmful, paranoia-driven thoughts toward healthier, more rational ones.

Incorporating self-reflection into a daily routine through digital tools allows individuals with PPD to engage in continuous learning and self-improvement. It also helps them track their progress as they develop a greater understanding of their condition. The convenience and accessibility of these resources mean that individuals can reflect on their experiences in real-time, whenever they choose. This regular practice not only fosters emotional awareness but also empowers individuals to take control of their mental health by reinforcing the belief that they can manage their thoughts and emotions. By using technology as a tool for self-reflection, individuals with PPD can gradually build emotional resilience, improve coping skills, and ultimately transform their relationship with their own thoughts.

The Rise of Virtual Support Groups

Virtual support groups have become a vital lifeline for individuals managing Paranoid Personality Disorder (PPD), offering a unique space for connection and shared understanding. These online groups, typically hosted on platforms like Zoom, Discord, or specialized mental health forums, allow individuals with PPD to come together, discuss their experiences, and offer each other mutual support. For those who often feel isolated or struggle with the social anxieties that accompany paranoia, virtual support groups can provide an essential sense of belonging and reassurance.

In these digital spaces, participants can discuss the challenges they face, exchange practical strategies for coping with paranoia, and share personal insights on navigating relationships, work, and daily life. Being part of a community that understands the nuances of PPD helps individuals feel validated, reducing the isolation that can often accompany mental health struggles. The support of others who genuinely comprehend the unique aspects of paranoia can be profoundly comforting and empowering, enabling individuals to feel less alone in their journey.

What makes virtual support groups even more effective is their accessibility and flexibility. Participants can join from the comfort of their own homes, removing the barriers of travel, scheduling conflicts, and in some cases, the stigma associated with attending in-person group sessions. For those who experience heightened anxiety in face-to-face interactions, virtual platforms allow them to engage at their own pace, feeling more in control of their involvement. Additionally, these groups often foster a more diverse community, with individuals from different regions and backgrounds connecting. This creates a broader network of shared experiences, helping individuals learn from others with varied perspectives.

Many virtual support groups are led by trained mental health professionals or peer counselors who guide discussions, ensuring that the environment remains safe, structured, and supportive. Facilitators help manage any conflicts that may arise, ensure that everyone has a voice, and provide evidence-based guidance when necessary. The presence of a professional or experienced peer helps reassure participants that they are receiving sound advice and emotional support, fostering trust in the group.

Ultimately, the rise of virtual support groups represents a significant shift in how individuals with PPD can access help. It creates a space where individuals can feel empowered to seek advice, share struggles, and celebrate successes without the traditional barriers that may have previously hindered them. These online communities offer an invaluable resource for managing PPD, promoting connection, healing, and the development of coping strategies in a supportive, inclusive environment.

Apps for Managing Anxiety and Paranoia

In recent years, a variety of mobile applications have been developed to assist individuals in managing anxiety and paranoia—common symptoms of Paranoid Personality Disorder (PPD). These apps offer practical tools that promote mental well-being, focusing on relaxation, mindfulness, cognitive restructuring, and emotional regulation. These apps not only help reduce immediate anxiety but also support long-term mental health improvement.

Some of the most widely used apps for managing anxiety and paranoia include:

- **Headspace** and **Calm**: These apps are designed to promote relaxation and mindfulness. They offer guided meditation, breathing exercises, and sleep aids that help users relax, calm their minds, and manage anxiety. These resources are especially beneficial for individuals with PPD, as they provide structured ways to focus the mind and reduce excessive worry.

- **Pacifica** and **Moodfit**: These apps are grounded in Cognitive Behavioral Therapy (CBT) techniques, making them particularly useful for individuals with paranoia. They offer tools to help users challenge negative thought patterns, reframe irrational beliefs, and track their moods over time. Pacifica also includes features for journaling, tracking stressors, and setting mental health goals, which can be valuable for those managing paranoia-related emotions.

- **CBT Thought Record Apps**: There are several apps specifically designed to help users track and challenge their thoughts, such as **CBT Thought Record Diary**. These apps guide users through the process of identifying distorted thinking and replacing it with more balanced, rational thoughts. This is particularly useful for those with PPD, as it helps break the cycle of paranoia by challenging the beliefs that fuel distrust and suspicion.

These apps are typically user-friendly, offering tailored experiences based on individual needs. Some apps allow users to:

- Log daily moods, tracking changes in emotional states and identifying patterns related to anxiety or paranoia.
- Document stressful events or triggers, helping individuals better understand their experiences and the factors that exacerbate their symptoms.
- Set goals for managing anxiety or improving mental well-being, offering structured pathways to create lasting positive change.

What makes these apps especially valuable is their accessibility and convenience. Most of them can be used anytime and anywhere, which means individuals can have immediate access to resources for managing overwhelming emotions in real time. Whether at work, home, or in public, users can engage with these tools to regain control of their emotional states, reduce anxiety, and develop healthier coping strategies.

Additionally, the ability to track progress over time empowers individuals to see the positive changes they've made in managing their mental health. This ongoing documentation can be encouraging and motivating, reinforcing the notion that managing anxiety and paranoia is not only possible but a step-by-step process that requires active engagement and self-compassion.

Incorporating these apps into a daily routine can complement traditional therapy and support overall mental health management. They offer a practical, low-cost resource for individuals with PPD to enhance their coping strategies and build resilience against anxiety and paranoia.

Ethical Considerations in Using Technology for Mental Health

While technology has revolutionized the way mental health care is accessed and managed, it also introduces several ethical concerns that need to be addressed to ensure the well-being of users. As individuals with Paranoid Personality Disorder (PPD) turn to digital platforms for support, it is crucial to consider privacy, data security, the quality of resources, and the balance between digital tools and traditional therapy. These factors must be carefully evaluated to ensure that technology is used effectively and responsibly in managing mental health.

1. Privacy and Data Security

One of the most pressing ethical issues when using technology for mental health is **privacy**. Many mental health apps and online therapy platforms require individuals to share sensitive personal information, such as mental health history, emotional states, and personal experiences. With this information being collected digitally, there is always a risk that it could be exposed or misused.

- **Data protection**: It is essential that platforms adhere to rigorous data protection laws, ensuring that all personal information is stored securely, and that users' privacy is respected at all times.
- **Transparency**: Digital platforms must be transparent about how they collect, store, and use user data. This includes providing clear terms of service and privacy policies that outline how data is shared, who has access to it, and the purpose for which it is used.

Users should carefully review the privacy policies of any mental health app or online therapy service they use, ensuring that the platform is compliant with regulations such as GDPR or HIPAA, which protect user data.

2. Quality and Accuracy of Mental Health Resources

Another ethical concern is the quality and accuracy of the resources provided through technology. Not all digital platforms are held to the same standards, and some may offer unverified or even harmful advice. This can be especially problematic for individuals with PPD, as inaccurate information could exacerbate feelings of paranoia or reinforce unhelpful thought patterns.

- **Evidence-based content**: Individuals should prioritize platforms that provide evidence-based resources, meaning the content is backed by research and proven to be effective in managing mental health.
- **Licensed professionals**: It is essential to ensure that any therapy or counseling services are delivered by licensed professionals with expertise in the field of mental health. This ensures that users are receiving appropriate and responsible care.

When engaging with online resources, individuals with PPD should be cautious of platforms or forums that offer generalized or anecdotal advice, as these may not be helpful or appropriate for managing a complex condition like paranoia.

3. Technology as a Supplement, Not a Substitute

While digital tools offer significant benefits, it is important to remember that they should not be seen as a replacement for in-person therapy or professional intervention. Technology can be a valuable supplement to traditional therapy, providing additional support, tracking tools, and educational resources. However, it cannot replace the personalized, in-depth care that a licensed therapist can provide in face-to-face sessions.

- **Complementary use**: Digital platforms should be used alongside regular therapy, not as a sole source of care. They can help individuals manage symptoms between appointments or serve as a tool for self-reflection and growth.
- **Professional guidance**: In cases of crisis or when symptoms of PPD become overwhelming, it is crucial to seek help from a licensed professional. Technology should not be a substitute for immediate or intensive therapeutic intervention.

It's important that users strike a balance between utilizing digital resources and continuing their journey with traditional mental health care.

In conclusion, the integration of technology into mental health management offers significant potential for individuals with Paranoid Personality Disorder. With access to online resources, digital therapy options, virtual support groups, and anxiety-management apps, individuals can gain valuable tools to better understand and cope with their condition. However, ethical considerations—particularly regarding privacy, the quality of information, and the role of technology in therapy—must be carefully considered. By ensuring privacy is respected, prioritizing accurate and professional content, and maintaining a balance between technology and traditional therapy, individuals with PPD can harness the power of digital tools to enhance their well-being while safeguarding their mental health.

Embracing technology in mental health care offers many opportunities for personal growth and empowerment, but it is essential that users engage with these tools mindfully and responsibly. With careful consideration, technology can complement the healing process, offering a path to better mental health for individuals with Paranoid Personality Disorder.

Chapter 13: Paranoia and the Aging Population

As people age, they undergo a series of changes, both physical and emotional, that can influence their mental and psychological well-being. These changes, which can include shifts in health, lifestyle, and personal relationships, may bring about new challenges that affect an individual's ability to cope with the world around them. One such challenge that may arise or become more pronounced with age is paranoia. For older adults, this may not simply be a product of individual temperament, but can also be influenced by the natural aging process.

Several factors contribute to the development or intensification of paranoid symptoms in older adults. Cognitive decline, for example, can lead to confusion, memory loss, and difficulty processing information, which in turn may cause individuals to become suspicious of others' intentions or actions. The loss of independence that often accompanies aging, such as needing assistance with daily activities or facing limitations in mobility, can also trigger feelings of vulnerability, leading to increased mistrust. Furthermore, as older adults experience changing social roles—such as retirement or the death of close family members or friends—the loss of familiar routines and support systems can cause feelings of isolation, further contributing to paranoia.

It is crucial to understand the relationship between aging and paranoid symptoms because this knowledge can help in identifying potential issues early and providing more effective care. Paranoia in older adults may not always look the same as it does in younger individuals. While it can involve similar suspicions or beliefs that others are plotting against them, in older adults, paranoia may stem more from confusion, anxiety, or fear of being taken advantage of. Understanding these nuances is essential for caregivers, family members, and healthcare providers who aim to provide compassionate and appropriate support.

This chapter delves into the complexities of paranoia in the aging population, highlighting how cognitive and emotional changes intersect with the manifestation of paranoid symptoms. It also explores how to recognize these symptoms in older adults, along with effective strategies for managing and supporting individuals who may experience paranoia. By taking a comprehensive approach, this chapter emphasizes how both caregivers and loved ones can play a pivotal role in improving the well-being of older individuals dealing with paranoia and related challenges.

The Relationship Between Aging and Paranoid Symptoms

Aging brings a series of life changes that can significantly impact an individual's emotional and mental well-being. These changes can include retirement, the loss of loved ones, declining physical health, and shifting social roles. For older adults, these factors can contribute to feelings of anxiety, insecurity, and isolation, which, in turn, may trigger or exacerbate paranoid thoughts. As a result, older adults may experience increased distrust, suspicion, or a belief that others are trying to deceive or harm them.

Key factors linking aging with paranoid symptoms include:

- **Retirement**: The loss of a career can lead to a loss of purpose and routine, triggering feelings of inadequacy and vulnerability, which may manifest as suspicion or paranoia.
- **Loss of loved ones**: The death of friends, family, or spouses can lead to emotional isolation, heightening feelings of mistrust and increasing paranoia about the reliability of others.

- **Declining physical health**: Chronic illnesses, disability, or reduced independence can foster a sense of dependence on others, which may contribute to fears of being taken advantage of or harmed.
- **Changes in social roles**: Retirement and the redefinition of one's role in family or community can lead to anxiety about one's place in the world, sometimes resulting in paranoid ideation.

For older adults with Paranoid Personality Disorder (PPD), the manifestation of paranoid symptoms may differ from those seen in younger individuals. While younger individuals with PPD may experience more overt and intense paranoid ideations, older adults often display more subtle forms of suspicion. These can include:

- **Excessive caution**: Older individuals may become hyper-vigilant or overly cautious in social or financial situations, driven by a belief that others are out to deceive or harm them.
- **Heightened vulnerability**: There may be a noticeable increase in feelings of being at the mercy of others, leading to a lack of trust or an overly defensive stance.
- **Social withdrawal**: As paranoia increases, older adults may isolate themselves more, avoiding social interactions out of fear or mistrust.

Furthermore, paranoia in older adults often overlaps with or is compounded by other age-related conditions, making diagnosis and treatment more complex. Some of the most common conditions associated with paranoia in older adults include:

- **Dementia**: Cognitive decline due to conditions like Alzheimer's disease can cause confusion and memory loss, leading individuals to misinterpret others' actions as threatening or harmful.
- **Depression**: Feelings of hopelessness or worthlessness in depression can often coincide with paranoid thoughts, leading individuals to believe they are being unfairly treated or targeted by others.
- **Medical conditions**: Certain illnesses or medications can also contribute to confusion or altered perceptions, which may amplify paranoia.

In conclusion, the relationship between aging and paranoid symptoms is complex. Age-related changes in physical health, social roles, and cognitive function can exacerbate or even trigger paranoid thoughts, making it crucial to understand the nuances of paranoia in older adults. Recognizing the overlap with other health conditions can lead to more effective treatment and support for older individuals dealing with these challenges.

Recognizing PPD in Older Adults

Diagnosing Paranoid Personality Disorder (PPD) in older adults presents unique challenges. Many of the symptoms of PPD overlap with age-related issues, such as cognitive decline or depression, making it difficult to distinguish between these conditions. Additionally, some level of suspicion or mistrust can be a normal part of aging, particularly when individuals face health challenges, physical decline, or the loss of independence.

However, recognizing PPD in older adults requires careful attention to the pattern and intensity of their behaviors, as well as understanding the difference between age-related concerns and pathological paranoia. The symptoms of PPD in older adults typically involve persistent, unfounded beliefs or behaviors that go beyond normal age-related concerns. Key indicators of PPD may include:

- **Excessive mistrust or suspicion**: Individuals with PPD may have a continuous belief that others have malicious or ulterior motives, even when there is no evidence to support such beliefs. For example, they may suspect that family

members or caregivers are trying to steal from
them or harm them.

- **Difficulty trusting others**: A person with PPD
  often refuses to confide in anyone, including
  family, friends, or caregivers, due to an
  overwhelming fear of betrayal or exploitation.
  This lack of trust can hinder their ability to
  engage in meaningful relationships or accept help
  when needed.

- **Hypervigilance**: Older adults with PPD may
  exhibit a heightened sense of alertness,
  constantly scanning their environment for
  potential threats. This may lead them to regularly
  seek reassurance or question the motives of
  others, even in situations that are safe or
  non-threatening.

- **Misinterpretation of social cues**: They may
  frequently overreact to neutral or benign
  interactions, perceiving ordinary behaviors or
  comments as hostile, critical, or threatening. For
  instance, they might believe that a caregiver's
  tone is condescending or that a family member is
  deliberately withholding information.

- **Emotional distance or detachment**: Fear of being hurt or deceived can make it difficult for individuals with PPD to form close, trusting relationships. As a result, they may appear emotionally distant, detached, or aloof, avoiding social interactions or rejecting attempts at intimacy, even from loved ones.

It is essential to differentiate between age-related cognitive decline and the long-standing patterns of paranoia associated with PPD. Cognitive impairment, which may result from dementia or other neurodegenerative conditions, can sometimes lead to confusion, memory loss, and anxiety. However, these symptoms are often episodic or fluctuating, whereas PPD is characterized by consistent, enduring patterns of suspicion and distrust.

A thorough mental health evaluation is necessary to distinguish between PPD and other conditions that may contribute to paranoia in older adults. This evaluation may include:

1. A **medical history** review to assess any physical health issues that could be affecting cognitive function.
2. A **cognitive assessment** to check for signs of dementia or other neurological disorders.

3. A **psychological evaluation** to assess the nature of the suspicious thoughts and behaviors and determine whether they align with the diagnostic criteria for PPD.

By carefully distinguishing between PPD and other conditions, healthcare providers can offer more targeted and effective support to older adults experiencing paranoia.

The Role of Dementia and Paranoia

Dementia, a condition characterized by progressive cognitive decline, is a common challenge among older adults. It can affect memory, thinking, and behavior, leading to a variety of symptoms, including paranoia. The relationship between dementia and paranoia is multifaceted, and it is crucial to understand how cognitive changes in dementia can contribute to suspicious or delusional thinking. Paranoia in individuals with dementia is not only a result of their cognitive impairment but also a response to the confusion and disorientation they experience as their mental faculties decline.

In the early stages of dementia, individuals may begin to show subtle signs of paranoia, which can gradually intensify as the disease progresses. The reasons behind these paranoid thoughts are often linked to changes in brain function, which can impair judgment, memory, and the ability to differentiate between reality and imagination. For example, an individual with dementia may struggle to recall where they left an item and, without realizing it, assume that someone else has stolen it. Similarly, they might develop irrational fears about their caregivers or family members, believing that these trusted individuals are intentionally trying to harm or exploit them.

Paranoia in individuals with dementia can manifest in various ways:

- **Beliefs of theft or mistreatment**: A common form of dementia-related paranoia is the belief that caregivers, family members, or friends are stealing from the individual or mistreating them. Even in the absence of any evidence, these accusations may become persistent, leading to tension and mistrust in relationships.

- **False accusations of betrayal**: Due to memory loss and confusion, individuals with dementia may falsely accuse loved ones of betrayal or disloyalty. These accusations can stem from a distorted memory of past events or an inability to remember recent interactions, which then get misinterpreted as betrayal.

- **Increased anxiety and agitation**: Paranoia in dementia often comes with heightened anxiety and emotional distress. Individuals may become agitated, especially when they are faced with unfamiliar situations, places, or people. This anxiety is exacerbated when they cannot process what is happening around them, leaving them feeling vulnerable and unsafe.

As dementia progresses, paranoia tends to worsen, particularly as cognitive functions continue to decline. This can lead to greater dependency on caregivers, as the individual feels more confused and fearful. Their ability to discern trustworthy people from potential threats may diminish, making them increasingly reliant on others for reassurance and support. For caregivers and family members, managing paranoia in dementia patients requires immense patience, compassion, and understanding.

Addressing paranoia in individuals with dementia involves:

- **Minimizing confusion**: Ensuring that the environment is familiar and predictable can help reduce feelings of anxiety and paranoia. A structured daily routine, clear communication, and the presence of familiar objects or people can provide a sense of security.

- **Offering reassurance**: When paranoia surfaces, caregivers should offer gentle reassurance, avoiding confrontation or dismissing the individual's fears. A calm and understanding approach can help soothe their anxiety and reduce the intensity of paranoid thoughts.

- **Redirecting attention**: In some cases, it can be helpful to redirect the individual's attention away from the source of paranoia. Engaging in a familiar activity, such as looking through a photo album or listening to music, can help shift their focus and reduce agitation.

- **Seeking professional guidance**: When paranoia becomes particularly distressing or difficult to manage, it is important to seek professional help. Healthcare providers can offer strategies for managing dementia-related paranoia and, in some cases, recommend medication to help alleviate symptoms.

Ultimately, addressing paranoia in individuals with dementia requires a compassionate, patient, and structured approach that focuses on creating a supportive environment. By recognizing the signs of paranoia and understanding the underlying cognitive changes, caregivers can help reduce distress and improve the quality of life for those living with dementia.

Coping Strategies for Older Adults with Paranoia

Paranoia can be distressing for older adults, but various coping strategies can help mitigate its impact and enhance their overall well-being. These strategies focus on creating stability, fostering trust, and promoting emotional and mental resilience. With the right support and tools, older adults can navigate feelings of paranoia more effectively while maintaining a sense of control and dignity in their lives.

Key Strategies for Coping with Paranoia in Older Adults

1. **Establishing a Consistent Routine**

    o A predictable daily schedule provides a sense of security and reduces uncertainty, which can exacerbate paranoid thoughts.

- Regular meal times, structured activities, and consistent sleeping patterns help create a stable and reassuring environment.

2. **Using Cognitive-Behavioral Techniques**

- Guided discussions can help older adults identify and challenge irrational or distorted thoughts in a supportive, non-confrontational manner.
- Reality-based exercises, such as gently reviewing evidence together, can assist in recognizing when fears are unfounded.

3. **Practicing Mindfulness and Relaxation**

- Mindfulness techniques, such as meditation, deep breathing, or progressive muscle relaxation, can reduce anxiety and promote emotional balance.
- Encouraging daily mindfulness exercises helps older adults remain present and less preoccupied with worrisome thoughts.

4. **Encouraging Social Engagement**

- Participation in social activities can counteract the isolation and loneliness that often fuel paranoia.

- Activities such as joining a local club, attending group events, or spending time with family can foster trust and connection.
- Support groups specifically tailored for older adults can provide a safe space to share experiences and learn coping strategies from peers.

5. **Creating a Safe and Familiar Environment**

- Ensuring the living space is secure, well-organized, and familiar helps reduce confusion and feelings of vulnerability.
- Practical measures, such as labeling items, using visual cues, and installing safety devices, can provide reassurance and a sense of control.
- Reducing clutter and maintaining a calm atmosphere minimizes potential triggers for anxiety or mistrust.

6. **Engaging in Hobbies and Meaningful Activities**

- Encouraging older adults to participate in activities they enjoy, such as gardening, art, or reading, can shift their focus away from paranoid thoughts.

- Structured activities that provide a sense of accomplishment can improve mood and build confidence.

7. **Promoting Physical Health**

- Regular exercise, a balanced diet, and adequate sleep are essential for mental and emotional well-being.
- Physical activities, such as walking, yoga, or light stretching, can reduce stress and improve mood.

Supporting Dignity and Independence

It's crucial for older adults to feel a sense of agency and control over their lives. Providing choices and encouraging their involvement in decision-making helps maintain their dignity while managing paranoia. Caregivers and family members should approach these strategies with patience and empathy, emphasizing reassurance without dismissing concerns. Small, positive actions, such as celebrating successes or offering gentle encouragement, can make a significant difference in empowering older adults to cope with paranoia effectively.

By addressing paranoia with a holistic and compassionate approach, older adults can achieve greater emotional stability and lead more fulfilling lives.

Family and Caregiver Support for Aging Individuals

Family members and caregivers play a crucial role in supporting older adults experiencing paranoia. This support requires a combination of empathy, patience, and understanding, as well as the ability to set healthy boundaries and encourage professional intervention when necessary. Recognizing that paranoia is often a symptom of deeper emotional or cognitive distress, rather than a personal attack, is key to fostering a supportive and effective caregiving environment.

Key Strategies for Caregivers and Family Members

1. **Active Listening**

    - Listen attentively to the concerns of the older adult without interrupting, judging, or dismissing their feelings.
    - Acknowledge their emotions by offering calm and reassuring responses, which can help reduce feelings of isolation and mistrust.

- Avoid arguments or attempts to immediately disprove their suspicions, as this may escalate anxiety.

2. **Clear and Transparent Communication**

   - Use simple, straightforward language when explaining situations or making plans.
   - Be consistent in actions and words to build trust, as vague or ambiguous statements can be misinterpreted and feed paranoia.
   - Provide regular updates on schedules, routines, or decisions to help reduce uncertainty and foster a sense of security.

3. **Establishing Healthy Boundaries**

   - While it is essential to provide support, caregivers must avoid enabling behaviors that could lead to excessive dependency or control.
   - Set clear, compassionate limits on how much reassurance or assistance is provided to ensure balance in the relationship.

4. **Encouraging Professional Help**

- Suggest therapy or counseling from licensed mental health professionals who specialize in paranoia or related conditions.
- Facilitate access to medical evaluations, particularly if underlying conditions like dementia or depression may be contributing to the paranoia.
- Support participation in support groups or community programs where individuals can connect with others who share similar experiences.

5. **Creating a Safe and Predictable Environment**

- Ensure that the living space is calm, organized, and familiar, as this can reduce confusion and anxiety.
- Use reminders, labels, or visual cues to help the individual feel more in control of their environment.

6. **Prioritizing Self-Care for Caregivers**

- Caring for someone with paranoia can be emotionally and physically exhausting, making self-care essential.
- Caregivers should take breaks, engage in their own hobbies, and seek support from

friends, family, or professional resources to prevent burnout.
  - Joining caregiver support groups can provide an outlet to share experiences and learn coping strategies from others in similar roles.

Building Trust and Resilience

Supporting an older adult with paranoia requires consistent efforts to build trust while respecting their autonomy. Offering reassurance without dismissing their concerns, maintaining a calm demeanor, and showing empathy can go a long way in fostering a positive relationship. At the same time, caregivers should gently guide the individual toward activities or therapies that promote mental well-being and reduce distress.

Paranoia in older adults presents unique challenges, but with compassionate and informed care, it is possible to improve their quality of life. By recognizing the signs of paranoia, understanding its relationship with aging and conditions like dementia, and employing tailored coping strategies, caregivers can help aging individuals feel safe and understood. Equally important is the caregiver's ability to prioritize their own well-being to sustain their ability to provide effective support. With a thoughtful and balanced approach, older adults experiencing

paranoia can maintain their dignity and continue to lead
meaningful lives.

Chapter 14: New Insights and Innovations in Treating Paranoid Personality Disorder

The understanding and treatment of Paranoid Personality Disorder (PPD) are advancing steadily, offering renewed hope for individuals living with this complex condition. With the growing body of research in mental health and the integration of innovative technologies, new approaches are emerging that aim to address PPD more comprehensively and effectively. These advances go beyond symptom management, focusing on understanding the root causes of paranoia, enhancing diagnostic accuracy, and tailoring interventions to meet the unique needs of each individual.

Groundbreaking studies in personality disorders have deepened insights into the interplay of genetic, neurological, and environmental factors that contribute to the development of PPD. Researchers are uncovering how early life experiences, brain function, and cognitive patterns shape the persistent mistrust and suspicion characteristic of the disorder. These findings are opening doors to more targeted therapeutic options.

In parallel, innovations in therapy and treatment methods are transforming the way PPD is managed. Emerging techniques such as neurofeedback and Eye Movement Desensitization and Reprocessing (EMDR) are offering alternative pathways for healing, especially for individuals resistant to traditional talk therapy. Advances in psychopharmacology are also expanding medication options, providing relief from severe symptoms and enhancing overall treatment outcomes.

The future of PPD treatment lies in personalized care, where interventions are tailored to the individual's specific needs, preferences, and life circumstances. This includes leveraging genetic testing, digital tools, and behavioral profiling to create a holistic and effective treatment plan. Additionally, the growing role of peer support programs highlights the importance of fostering community and mutual understanding in the recovery process.

As research and innovation continue to push boundaries, the landscape of mental health care is being reshaped. This chapter delves into these developments, offering a glimpse into the potential of these advancements to provide individuals with PPD greater opportunities for healing, empowerment, and improved quality of life.

Breakthrough Research in Paranoia and Personality Disorders

Recent advancements in research are unraveling the complexities of paranoia and personality disorders, offering deeper insights into the causes and manifestations of conditions like Paranoid Personality Disorder (PPD). By exploring the interplay of genetic, neurobiological, and environmental factors, scientists are gaining a clearer picture of the mechanisms that drive paranoid thought patterns and behaviors.

Key Areas of Breakthrough Research:

1. **Genetic and Neurological Contributions**
   Cutting-edge neuroimaging studies have identified significant structural and functional differences in the brains of individuals with PPD. Notably, areas such as the amygdala, which processes fear and threat perception, and the prefrontal cortex, responsible for rational thinking and decision-making, show altered activity. These findings suggest that heightened sensitivity to perceived threats may have a

biological basis, providing a foundation for more targeted treatments.

2. **Impact of Early-Life Experiences**
   Research highlights the profound influence of early trauma, neglect, and abuse in shaping the paranoid worldview often seen in PPD. These formative experiences can instill deep-seated mistrust and foster maladaptive coping mechanisms that persist into adulthood. Understanding these roots underscores the importance of therapeutic interventions that address unresolved emotional wounds and foster healthier patterns of trust and communication.

3. **Cognitive and Behavioral Patterns**
   Studies are refining our understanding of how cognitive distortions, such as overgeneralization and catastrophizing, contribute to paranoia. Individuals with PPD tend to misinterpret neutral or ambiguous situations as threatening, reinforcing their suspicion of others. Behavioral research is helping identify these thought processes, paving the way for cognitive-behavioral therapies tailored to the unique challenges of PPD.

4. **Environmental Influences and Social Dynamics**

   Beyond genetics and personal history, environmental factors like social isolation and chronic stress can amplify paranoid tendencies. Research is exploring how these external pressures interact with biological predispositions, offering insights into preventative measures and community-based interventions.

These findings represent a significant step forward, bridging the gap between theoretical research and practical application. By deepening our understanding of the biological, psychological, and environmental underpinnings of PPD, this research is paving the way for innovative, personalized approaches to treatment that prioritize the unique needs of each individual.

Advances in Psychopharmacology for Treating Paranoia

Advancements in psychopharmacology are opening new avenues for managing paranoia in individuals with Paranoid Personality Disorder (PPD). While psychotherapy remains the primary approach to addressing the underlying patterns of thought and behavior, medication can play a vital supportive role in mitigating severe symptoms like anxiety, agitation, or persistent mistrust. Modern developments in this field aim to offer more targeted and effective pharmacological interventions, improving overall outcomes for patients.

Key Advances in Psychopharmacology:

1. **Antipsychotic Medications**
   Atypical antipsychotics, including aripiprazole and risperidone, have shown promise in reducing paranoia by regulating dopamine activity in the brain. These medications help to stabilize mood and diminish exaggerated threat perceptions, which are often at the core of paranoid thinking. Their improved side-effect profile compared to older antipsychotics makes them a safer option for long-term use.

2. **Anti-Anxiety Medications**
   Anxiety frequently exacerbates paranoid symptoms, creating a vicious cycle of heightened suspicion and distress. Medications like benzodiazepines provide short-term relief from acute anxiety, while selective serotonin reuptake inhibitors (SSRIs), such as sertraline or escitalopram, offer longer-term benefits by balancing serotonin levels. These interventions can help patients feel calmer, which in turn may reduce their reliance on defensive or suspicious

behaviors.

3. **Emerging Pharmacological Innovations**
   Research is uncovering new pathways to address
   paranoia more directly. Experimental drugs
   targeting specific neural circuits involved in
   threat detection and emotional regulation are
   currently in development. These medications aim
   to correct the overactivation of brain areas like
   the amygdala, providing more precise and
   effective treatment options in the future.

4. **Individualized Medication Plans**
   The push toward personalized medicine has led
   to tailored approaches for managing paranoia. By
   considering genetic, biological, and
   psychological factors, clinicians can create
   medication plans that align with an individual's
   unique needs. This minimizes side effects and
   increases the likelihood of adherence to
   treatment.

Challenges and Considerations:

Despite these advancements, careful monitoring remains
crucial. Paranoid individuals may view medication or the
treatment process itself with suspicion, complicating
adherence. Open communication, patient education, and

building trust between healthcare providers and patients are essential to ensuring successful outcomes.

Incorporating pharmacological strategies into a broader treatment plan offers new hope for individuals with PPD. By addressing the physiological components of paranoia alongside therapeutic interventions, these innovations provide a more comprehensive path toward recovery and improved quality of life.

Emerging Therapies: Neurofeedback and EMDR

Innovative therapies such as neurofeedback and Eye Movement Desensitization and Reprocessing (EMDR) are emerging as promising options in the treatment of Paranoid Personality Disorder (PPD) and related conditions. These approaches offer non-invasive, personalized techniques that cater to individuals who may be resistant to conventional methods, focusing on addressing the root causes of paranoia rather than merely managing symptoms.

Neurofeedback: Enhancing Brain Regulation

Neurofeedback is a cutting-edge therapy that uses real-time feedback to help individuals regulate their brain activity. By monitoring brainwave patterns, participants learn to adjust their neural responses, fostering improved emotional control and cognitive stability.

For individuals with PPD, neurofeedback can be particularly effective in:

- **Reducing Hypervigilance**: By training the brain to respond less intensely to perceived threats, neurofeedback helps to diminish the constant state of alertness and suspicion that characterizes paranoia.
- **Improving Emotional Regulation**: Enhanced awareness of brain activity enables individuals to manage stress and anxiety more effectively, which are often key drivers of paranoid thought patterns.
- **Promoting a Sense of Control**: As participants observe their ability to influence their brain function, they often experience an increased sense of empowerment, counteracting feelings of helplessness or vulnerability.

EMDR: Reprocessing Traumatic Experiences

Eye Movement Desensitization and Reprocessing (EMDR) was originally developed to treat trauma but has shown significant potential in addressing paranoia, especially when rooted in past negative experiences.

EMDR involves guiding the individual through structured sets of eye movements while they recall distressing memories or fears. This process helps to reframe and reprocess these memories, reducing their emotional impact and altering maladaptive associations.

For individuals with PPD, EMDR can assist in:

- **Addressing Underlying Fears**: Many paranoid beliefs stem from past betrayals, traumas, or neglect. EMDR helps individuals process these experiences in a healthier way, diminishing their influence on current perceptions.
- **Building Resilience**: By reducing the emotional charge of distressing memories, EMDR allows individuals to face new situations with less suspicion and heightened trust.
- **Improving Relationships**: As negative associations fade, individuals may find it easier to form and maintain connections with others, mitigating the social isolation often linked to PPD.

The Appeal of Emerging Therapies

Both neurofeedback and EMDR cater to the increasing demand for holistic and personalized mental health treatments. Their non-invasive nature makes them appealing to individuals who are hesitant to engage in traditional therapy or medication-based approaches.

By targeting the underlying mechanisms of paranoia and fostering long-term emotional and cognitive improvements, these therapies offer a transformative path forward for individuals with PPD. As research and clinical experience with these methods grow, they hold the potential to become integral components of comprehensive treatment plans.

The Future of Personalized Treatment Approaches

The future of treating Paranoid Personality Disorder (PPD) is shifting toward personalized medicine, where interventions are tailored to the specific needs, preferences, and characteristics of each individual. This evolving approach prioritizes precision, taking into account a variety of biological, psychological, and social factors to deliver more effective and sustainable outcomes. By moving away from one-size-fits-all solutions, clinicians are better equipped to address the complexities of PPD, fostering improved recovery and overall well-being.

Key Advancements in Personalized Treatment

1. Genetic Insights Driving Medication Choices

The incorporation of genetic testing into mental health care is revolutionizing pharmacological treatment. By analyzing a person's genetic makeup, clinicians can identify how they are likely to metabolize certain medications. This approach helps in:

- **Minimizing Side Effects**: Tailored prescriptions reduce the likelihood of adverse reactions.
- **Maximizing Effectiveness**: Clinicians can select medications that align with an individual's genetic profile, improving symptom management.

For individuals with PPD, this means a reduced trial-and-error period in finding the right medication, which is particularly valuable for those who may already harbor mistrust toward treatment.

2. Behavioral Profiling for Targeted Interventions

Advanced techniques in behavioral analysis allow for a deeper understanding of an individual's thought processes, emotional triggers, and coping mechanisms. Through comprehensive assessments, clinicians can:

- Identify specific patterns of paranoia, mistrust, or hypervigilance.

- Develop therapy plans that address the unique
  cognitive distortions and fears associated with
  PPD.
  This level of precision enables the creation of
  therapies that resonate more effectively with the
  individual's experiences and mindset.

3. Integrating Technology for Continuous Support

The integration of technology into mental health care is
expanding access to personalized support. Apps and
digital platforms now play a crucial role in monitoring
symptoms and facilitating communication between
patients and clinicians. Some features include:

- **Symptom Tracking**: Individuals can log their
  thoughts, emotions, and behaviors, providing
  valuable insights into their progress.
- **Real-Time Feedback**: Digital tools offer
  prompts and exercises to help manage paranoia
  or anxiety in the moment.
- **Enhanced Connectivity**: Therapists can stay
  updated on a patient's condition between
  sessions, enabling more responsive care.

This technological evolution empowers individuals with
PPD to take an active role in their treatment, fostering a
sense of autonomy and collaboration.

A Holistic Vision for Personalized Care

The future of treatment for PPD lies in combining these advancements to address the full spectrum of an individual's needs. A holistic approach considers:

- **Biological Factors**: Genetic predispositions, neurobiological patterns, and physical health.
- **Psychological Components**: Thought distortions, emotional resilience, and coping skills.
- **Social Influences**: Relationships, environmental stressors, and support systems.

By weaving these elements into a cohesive plan, clinicians can provide care that not only alleviates symptoms but also empowers individuals to lead more fulfilling lives. The evolution of personalized treatment heralds a new era of hope for those navigating the challenges of PPD, ensuring that their journey toward recovery is as unique as they are.

The Role of Peer Support in Recovery

Peer support has emerged as a vital component in the recovery process for individuals with Paranoid Personality Disorder (PPD). It provides a unique form of connection that goes beyond clinical treatment, offering a space where individuals can share experiences, foster mutual understanding, and build resilience. By engaging with others who have navigated similar struggles, those with PPD can find a sense of belonging that helps to counteract feelings of isolation often associated with the condition.

Benefits of Peer Support

1. **Empowerment Through Shared Experiences**

   - Hearing about the journeys and successes of peers who have managed PPD can instill hope and motivation.
   - Personal stories of overcoming challenges provide a roadmap for others, inspiring active participation in their own recovery.

2. **Validation and Understanding**

   - Peers offer a level of empathy that professionals may struggle to match, as they intimately understand the emotions and thought patterns associated with PPD.
   - This shared understanding creates a judgment-free environment where individuals feel seen and accepted.

3. **Opportunities for Skill Development**

- Peer groups serve as a safe space for practicing essential interpersonal skills, such as trust-building, communication, and conflict resolution.
- Role-playing and collaborative activities help participants work through relational challenges in a supportive setting.

Integrating Peer Support Into Treatment

Programs designed to include peer support have shown promise in enhancing recovery outcomes for those with PPD. These initiatives often take various forms, such as:

- **Facilitated Group Therapy**: Led by trained facilitators who guide discussions and ensure a constructive atmosphere.
- **Peer-Led Support Groups**: Meetings where individuals share experiences, offer advice, and provide encouragement.
- **Online Communities and Forums**: Digital platforms that allow individuals to connect with peers across the globe, offering accessibility and anonymity.

The Holistic Impact of Peer Support

Beyond individual benefits, peer support fosters a culture of collective resilience. Participants often transition from receiving help to offering it, which reinforces their own recovery while contributing to others' growth. This reciprocal dynamic helps build a strong, supportive community where everyone feels valued.

A New Horizon in PPD Treatment

The integration of peer support into treatment plans is part of a broader transformation in the approach to managing PPD. Alongside advancements in psychopharmacology, innovative therapies like neurofeedback, and personalized care strategies, peer support underscores the importance of addressing both the emotional and social dimensions of recovery.

By leveraging the power of shared experiences, mental health professionals can complement clinical interventions with a human-centered approach that empowers individuals with PPD to rebuild trust, foster meaningful relationships, and regain confidence in their ability to lead fulfilling lives. As peer support continues to gain recognition as an essential element of care, it paves the way for a more inclusive, compassionate, and effective mental health landscape.

Chapter 15: Living a Full Life with Paranoid Personality Disorder

Paranoid Personality Disorder (PPD) brings its own set of challenges, but it does not determine the limits of a person's potential for growth, happiness, and meaningful relationships. While the symptoms of PPD can be overwhelming at times, they do not have to overshadow the ability to live a fulfilling and rewarding life. With the right combination of understanding, strategies, and support, individuals with PPD can find strength in their journey and reclaim control over their lives.

Living with PPD requires more than just managing the symptoms—it is about creating a life that allows for both personal growth and connection with others. With dedication, a willingness to seek help, and a compassionate approach to oneself, individuals can move beyond the constraints of paranoia and build a life that is rich with meaning and possibility.

This chapter delves into the various steps and strategies that individuals with PPD can use to nurture their well-being. It highlights how to cultivate self-compassion, fight against societal stigma, maintain progress in recovery, and ultimately create a life that goes beyond the limitations imposed by paranoid thinking. Additionally, it explores how individuals can use their own experiences to inspire and empower others, creating a ripple effect of healing and support in their communities.

At the heart of this journey is the belief that with the right tools and mindset, it is possible to overcome the obstacles that PPD presents and live a life that is not defined by fear and suspicion, but instead by growth, connection, and empowerment. Through self-acceptance and resilience, individuals with PPD can create lasting change, not only in their own lives but also in the lives of those around them.

Embracing Self-Acceptance and Compassion

The path to living fully with Paranoid Personality Disorder (PPD) begins with embracing self-acceptance. It's essential to acknowledge that while PPD is a part of one's identity, it does not define who a person is in their entirety. Accepting oneself with compassion allows individuals to break free from the constraints of their symptoms and recognize their inherent worth. Instead of viewing PPD as a burden or flaw, it becomes an aspect to manage, understand, and navigate, not as something to be ashamed of.

Self-compassion is a powerful catalyst for healing, enabling individuals to replace harsh self-criticism with kindness and understanding. Embracing the idea that seeking help is a sign of strength, not weakness, fosters a sense of agency and self-respect. It is essential to remember that mental health challenges, including PPD, are part of the human experience, and reaching out for support is a courageous and necessary step toward growth.

Self-acceptance is nurtured when individuals celebrate even the smallest victories along their journey. Recognizing progress, no matter how incremental, reinforces the belief that change is possible. Every step toward managing symptoms—whether it's learning to trust a little more, reducing anxiety, or simply acknowledging emotional vulnerability—is a victory worth celebrating.

Reframing negative self-beliefs is another key aspect of self-acceptance. For many individuals with PPD, there may be a tendency to internalize feelings of inadequacy or inferiority. However, shifting the focus to positive affirmations and encouraging self-talk can transform those beliefs over time. Instead of viewing oneself through the lens of suspicion and fear, it's possible to adopt a more compassionate perspective that emphasizes personal strengths, resilience, and the capacity for growth.

Above all, patience plays a critical role in cultivating self-acceptance. Recovery and healing are not immediate processes, but rather ongoing journeys. By approaching their struggles with patience and understanding, individuals can avoid falling into the trap of frustration or discouragement. It's important to view setbacks as part of the process and to recognize that every effort, no matter how small, contributes to lasting change.

Through the practice of self-compassion, individuals with PPD can gradually dismantle the cycle of self-doubt and mistrust that often holds them back. With time, effort, and patience, they can learn to embrace their full selves—both the strengths and challenges—and walk forward with a sense of empowerment, confidence, and the belief that they are worthy of love, support, and a fulfilling life.

Overcoming the Shame and Stigma of Mental Health Issues

Overcoming the shame and stigma associated with mental health issues is a critical step toward healing and growth for individuals living with Paranoid Personality Disorder (PPD). For many, the social misconceptions about mental health can create a sense of isolation and embarrassment, which in turn makes seeking help more difficult. Yet, dismantling these barriers is not only possible but necessary for personal well-being and societal progress.

The first step in overcoming stigma is to acknowledge that mental health struggles are just as valid and significant as physical health challenges. Society tends to prioritize physical ailments over psychological ones, but mental health deserves the same level of care, attention, and respect. By embracing this truth, individuals can begin to see their experiences not as flaws or personal shortcomings, but as real, treatable health conditions that require support and understanding.

Education is a powerful tool in changing perceptions, and one of the most effective ways to combat stigma is through sharing personal stories. By speaking openly about PPD and its impact, individuals can help others see beyond the surface, revealing the complexities and humanity of those living with the disorder. Personal stories have the power to humanize mental health struggles and shift public attitudes from judgment to empathy. The more individuals with PPD engage in these conversations, the more society can collectively move toward a more compassionate, informed understanding of mental health.

Another vital strategy is to seek out and engage with supportive communities where acceptance replaces stigma. Being part of a group where mental health issues are openly discussed and understood can provide a sense of belonging and validation. These communities—whether in person or online—offer a safe space to share experiences, gain insights, and foster connections with others who truly understand. In these supportive environments, there is no need to hide or pretend, and individuals can feel empowered to embrace their journey toward healing without fear of judgment.

As public awareness continues to grow and mental health becomes a more widely accepted topic, individuals living with PPD can take pride in their resilience. Their experiences contribute to a broader movement aimed at destigmatizing mental health issues and promoting greater understanding across society. The act of openly confronting stigma not only empowers individuals but also creates a ripple effect, inspiring others to do the same.

By breaking free from the shame and stigma surrounding mental health, individuals with PPD can experience a profound sense of liberation. When they recognize their struggles as part of the shared human experience, they no longer have to carry the burden of isolation or silence. Instead, they can move forward with a renewed sense of pride in their resilience and a deeper connection to the world around them.

Strategies for Sustaining Long-Term Recovery

Sustaining long-term recovery from Paranoid Personality Disorder (PPD) requires commitment and consistent effort. It's a lifelong journey that demands patience, flexibility, and a proactive approach to managing symptoms while nurturing overall well-being. With the right strategies in place, recovery can be maintained in a way that fosters growth, stability, and personal empowerment.

One of the most effective strategies for sustaining recovery is establishing a routine. A predictable daily schedule creates a sense of stability and helps minimize the stress and anxiety that often accompany uncertainty. By integrating regular activities and healthy habits into daily life, individuals can manage their symptoms more effectively and reduce the unpredictability that may trigger feelings of paranoia or anxiety. Routine also provides a framework for personal growth, offering the structure needed to build confidence and maintain a steady course.

Continued therapy is also essential for long-term recovery. Regular sessions with a therapist allow individuals to maintain access to professional support, helping them stay on track and address any emerging challenges. Therapy provides a space to explore new coping strategies, refine existing ones, and gain insight into the emotional and cognitive patterns that may arise. It's important to recognize that therapy is not just for times of crisis—ongoing check-ins ensure that progress is monitored and that setbacks can be addressed in real time.

Building and nurturing a strong support network is another crucial aspect of sustaining recovery. Having trusted friends, family, and peers who understand the challenges of PPD can offer emotional safety and reduce the isolation that often accompanies the disorder. These connections provide an invaluable source of reassurance and validation, allowing individuals to feel supported and less vulnerable to the effects of paranoia. Being able to share experiences, ask for help, and offer support in return strengthens these relationships and reinforces the importance of community in the healing process.

Mindful self-care is a practice that promotes emotional balance and resilience. Engaging in activities like meditation, exercise, and journaling can help regulate emotions, reduce stress, and foster a sense of calm. These practices allow individuals to reconnect with themselves and cultivate a greater sense of self-awareness and control. Regular self-care routines also contribute to overall well-being by enhancing physical health and mental clarity, which in turn supports recovery from PPD.

Sustaining long-term recovery from PPD involves finding a balance between managing symptoms and nurturing emotional health. There will inevitably be setbacks, but these should be seen as opportunities for growth rather than failures. Each step forward—no matter how small—is a victory that should be celebrated, as it reinforces the progress made along the way. By maintaining a proactive mindset, embracing ongoing support, and prioritizing self-care, individuals can continue to build resilience and lead fulfilling lives despite the challenges they face.

How to Create a Life Beyond Paranoia

Creating a life beyond paranoia involves shifting the focus from the constraints of fear and suspicion to the limitless possibilities of personal growth, connection, and achievement. While paranoia may have shaped one's perception of the world, it doesn't have to dictate one's future. By redirecting energy toward positive experiences and aspirations, individuals can begin to redefine their lives and cultivate a sense of fulfillment that transcends the limitations of Paranoid Personality Disorder (PPD).

One powerful way to move beyond paranoia is by exploring new interests. Engaging in activities that spark curiosity or passion—whether it's picking up a new hobby, delving into creative projects, or volunteering—can bring a renewed sense of joy and purpose. These pursuits not only provide distraction from negative thoughts but also open up opportunities for personal growth and achievement. Whether through art, music, nature, or service to others, these endeavors can help individuals reconnect with what brings them joy, offering a sense of fulfillment that paranoia often obscures.

Setting achievable goals is another key element in creating a life beyond paranoia. Breaking down larger aspirations into small, manageable steps can help build momentum and confidence. Achieving these goals, no matter how minor they may seem, fosters a sense of accomplishment and reinforces the belief that personal growth is possible. Whether it's a career milestone, a fitness target, or learning a new skill, each accomplishment contributes to the broader vision of a fulfilling life. By setting clear, realistic goals, individuals can replace the feelings of inadequacy and fear often triggered by PPD with a more empowered sense of self-efficacy.

Fostering meaningful relationships is also essential for moving beyond paranoia. Building connections with others based on trust, empathy, and mutual respect provides a solid foundation for emotional well-being. These relationships, whether with family, friends, or new acquaintances, can help counter the isolation that often accompanies PPD. Engaging in open, honest communication and cultivating deep bonds with others can create a support system that offers both reassurance and connection. As these relationships strengthen, the sense of belonging and security grows, diminishing the influence of paranoia over time.

Living beyond paranoia isn't about eliminating fear entirely; it's about learning to navigate life with a sense of purpose, joy, and connection despite the challenges that may arise. By focusing on strengths, passions, and the potential for personal growth, individuals can move past the confines of PPD and create a meaningful, fulfilling life. Through intentional actions, self-compassion, and a commitment to nurturing relationships and goals, it is possible to rediscover the richness of life and embrace all the possibilities that lie ahead.

Moving Forward: Empowering Others with Paranoid Personality Disorder

Living with Paranoid Personality Disorder (PPD) can often feel isolating and overwhelming. However, it also provides unique insights and strengths that can be harnessed to empower others who are navigating similar challenges. The journey to recovery is not one to travel alone, and those who have faced the complexities of PPD can play a vital role in supporting and guiding others along their own paths. By sharing experiences, offering mentorship, and advocating for mental health awareness, individuals with PPD can create a ripple effect of healing and community-building that goes beyond their own personal growth.

Empowering others who are struggling with PPD can take many forms. One of the most impactful ways is by becoming a peer supporter. Many individuals living with mental health conditions often find comfort in connecting with someone who understands their experiences firsthand. As a peer supporter, sharing your own recovery journey can provide invaluable hope to others who may feel isolated or hopeless. Offering empathy, advice, and encouragement can help them navigate their own healing process, knowing they are not alone in their struggles.

Writing or speaking about personal recovery journeys is another powerful method of empowerment. Sharing stories of resilience and growth can inspire others to take the first step toward seeking help or continuing their recovery. Whether through blogs, articles, books, or public speaking engagements, telling one's story can break the silence surrounding mental health, reduce stigma, and spark important conversations. These narratives remind others that recovery is not only possible but achievable, no matter how difficult the journey may seem.

Another form of empowerment comes through collaborating with mental health professionals to improve resources and treatment approaches. People living with PPD possess unique perspectives that can help shape more effective therapeutic interventions and community resources. By working with clinicians, support groups, or advocacy organizations, individuals can contribute to the creation of tailored approaches that better serve those with PPD. This collaborative effort can also ensure that treatment remains relevant and compassionate, taking into account the lived experiences of those directly affected.

When individuals with PPD step into roles of leadership, advocacy, or mentorship, they not only help others but also find purpose, strength, and healing in their own journey. Taking an active role in the mental health community can be deeply fulfilling, as it offers opportunities for growth, self-expression, and connection. It is a reminder that even in the face of adversity, we can contribute positively to the lives of others while continuing our own healing process.

While Paranoid Personality Disorder presents unique obstacles, it does not have to define or limit an individual's potential for a meaningful and fulfilling life. By embracing self-acceptance, fostering connections, and building resilience, individuals with PPD can rewrite their narratives. Recovery from PPD is not a linear journey—it is a continuous process filled with steps forward, occasional setbacks, and ongoing learning. Each effort, whether through therapy, building relationships, or engaging in advocacy, contributes to a broader sense of empowerment and growth.

The path to healing is deeply personal, yet it is enriched by the shared experiences and collective strength of others walking the same road. By embracing the journey, seeking support, and empowering those around them, individuals with PPD can transform their challenges into opportunities for personal growth and positive impact. With perseverance, compassion, and a willingness to help others, life with PPD can become one of hope, meaning, and profound transformation.

Conclusion: A Final Word on Thriving Beyond Paranoia

Living with Paranoid Personality Disorder (PPD) undoubtedly presents significant challenges, yet it is important to remember that these challenges do not define an individual's worth or limit their potential. While paranoia can cloud perspectives and create barriers, it is not an insurmountable obstacle. With the right support, self-awareness, and commitment to healing, individuals living with PPD can discover a life filled with purpose, meaning, and connection—beyond the confines of their fears and mistrust.

The journey toward healing begins with self-compassion, acceptance, and understanding. Acknowledging that PPD is only a part of one's identity, and not the entirety of who they are, opens the door to self-discovery and growth. Recovery is not about eradicating all traces of paranoia, but about learning to live with it in a way that does not limit one's potential or joy. This is a lifelong journey that requires patience, resilience, and continuous effort. It is a journey that can be navigated with the support of loved ones, therapists, and communities that offer understanding and acceptance.

Furthermore, the act of breaking free from the stigma surrounding mental health is transformative. By choosing to speak openly about PPD, whether through personal narratives or public advocacy, individuals can help reduce the societal barriers that perpetuate shame and isolation. This not only fosters a more compassionate environment for others but also strengthens the individual's sense of identity and pride in their recovery journey.

Sustaining long-term recovery requires intentional practices that nurture emotional balance, create stability, and foster connection. Establishing a supportive routine, engaging in regular therapy, and prioritizing self-care are all critical components of maintaining mental health and well-being. Recovery is not a destination but a process—one that evolves as individuals learn new strategies for managing symptoms, building healthy relationships, and pursuing personal goals.

Ultimately, moving beyond paranoia involves shifting focus away from fear and mistrust and toward growth, purpose, and connection. It is about discovering new passions, setting achievable goals, and investing in relationships that bring joy and meaning. By nurturing one's strengths and embracing life's opportunities, individuals with PPD can redefine what is possible for their future.

Perhaps most importantly, by empowering others with similar experiences—whether through mentorship, advocacy, or shared stories—individuals with PPD contribute to a broader culture of empathy, understanding, and support. In doing so, they not only enrich their own lives but also inspire others to embark on their own healing journeys. Together, this shared strength creates a cycle of growth and hope that reverberates beyond individual experiences.

Thriving beyond paranoia is not only possible; it is a journey of immense personal growth, resilience, and transformation. By embracing self-compassion, connecting with others, and continuously working toward healing, those living with PPD can forge a life that is rich with possibility. It is a life that demonstrates that, no matter the challenges we face, there is always hope, and there is always room for growth, connection, and joy.